NT·INSTITUTE

LEBBEUS WOODS

Architectural Monographs No 22

LEBBEUS WOODS

ANARCHITECTURE: Architecture is a Political Act

A.D. ACADEMY EDITIONS / ST. MARTIN'S PRESS

TO ALEKSANDRA WAGNER

Architectural Monographs No 22
Editorial Offices
42 Leinster Gardens London W2 3AN

ISSN 0141-2191

Editorial and Design Team
Andreas Papadakis (Publisher)
Vivian Constantinopoulos (Senior Editor)
Andrea Bettella (Senior Designer), Annamarie Uhr (Design)

All drawings by Lebbeus Woods
Technical realisation of models by Christopher Otterbine, with Anik Pearson, Jorg Zander,
James Hicks and Herman Ventura
All model photography by Lebbeus Woods

Subscription Department
Mira Joka
42 Leinster Gardens London W2 3AN

Publisher's note
Although I had known about the work of Lebbeus Woods for several years, particularly from
seeing his work exhibited at the Deutsches Architekturmuseum in Frankfurt in 1989, it wasn't
until seeing his presentation at a conference which I organised at the Royal Academy in
London in 1991 that I was strongly impressed by the free spirit that dominates this architect's
work. The three-dimensionality of his new drawings and the force of the concepts discussed
by Woods were two aspects which particularly arrested my attention. He speaks of 'instrumental', rather than 'expressive' architecture and it is that which we can see conveyed in the
projects presented here: freespace structures, instrumental of a freedom of the individual,
initiating the heterarchy which Woods seeks. *ACP*

Cover: Drawing from the War and Architecture series, 1992; *p2:* Drawing from DMZ, 1988

First published in Great Britain in 1992 by
ACADEMY EDITIONS
An imprint of the Academy Group Ltd
a member of the VCH Publishing Group

ISBN 1 85490 148 6 (HB)
ISBN 1 85490 149 4 (PB)

Published in the United States of America in 1992 by
ST MARTIN'S PRESS
175 Fifth Avenue, New York, NY 10010

ISBN 0-312-08110-3 (HB)
ISBN 0-312-08111-1 (PB)

Printed and bound in Singapore

CONTENTS

AT THE OUTERMOST BOUNDARY

Is there a space for the tender hope that things will change for all those who still believe in change? For an optimism that holds back the glance towards the abyss? Or to put it in other words, does Lebbeus Woods allow us in his works to forget, for moments, the *terra incognita*, the crisis of awareness afflicting modern men, the sad reality of the present, and particularly that of architecture?

Of course, he is not a 'deconstructor', and he doesn't use the method of Deconstruction either as an excuse for laziness, or as an authorisation for an indifferent architectural expression. No! If there is an element of Deconstructivism in his work, it is not indecisiveness, but rather a criticism of existing architecture. Lebbeus Woods' criticism is shattering. He creates autonomous fields of force with his projects, murderously visionary images: real, frightening, and at the same time liberating. Flashes of light illuminating reality like lightning. In these projects, he throws images of yearning onto the world. It is an empty world, dominated by the cold luxury of its architecture, almost leaden — the alchemical intention of a visionary. A world made of raw iron, grey-washed, rusted and stained. An aesthetically overwhelming world, comparable to that of a cargo ship's hold, which only comes alive through provocation — the delusion of innovation opposing nostalgic languor.

To understand architecture as architecture always requires something superhuman. Lebbeus Woods, the metaphysical architect at the edge of architecture, accomplishes what is humanly possible, and at the outermost boundary. His 'mirror images' proscribe the conditions of an inevitable awakening, of a fusion of the ideal and the sensual, in visions which have become true.

He knows that urgency prevents certainty. This could be the reason he begins to build his urban constructions on paper. In the same way that light emerges from his wind-soaked ruins, Lebbeus Woods overcomes the border between dream and reality. *Peter Noever*

Director of the Osterreichisches Museum für Angewandte Kunst (Austrian Museum of Applied Arts) in Vienna, and Editor of Architecture In Transition *(published by Prestel, Munich)*

Crucial question — what is an inconsistent pattern? The cities of an experimental culture will be formed on inconsistent patterns, and will produce them. These will be their chief products, the result of a way of living driven by the need for clarity on shifting landscapes of the ephemeral.

Within the historical and hierarchical city, the heterarchical city — the free-zone — is constructed. This is one level of inconsistency. But there is a deeper one — within the heterarchical city, another city of unknown shape and substance is constructed — the city which cannot be named. Its inhabitants are those who do not fit patterns at all. Their names are known, but beg to be forgotten. Experimentalists in experience, they leave no forwarding address.

Politics of construction: who designs, who builds, who owns, who inhabits? The architect who designs building types is a pyramid builder, who follows the hidden forms already inscribed by those expressing and dominating others, and who benefit by conventions, conformity, and all adherence to the rules of the normative. The inhabitants are on the lowest level of the game. They receive what has been given, yet bear all the weight of the superstructure above. *Who are the inhabitants?*

The architect who designs building non-types — the freespaces of unknown purpose and meaning — inverts the pyramid and creates new ones. Each inhabitant is an apex, placed on end, a point of personal origin. Each pyramid expands into a void of time, seeking its base, its terminus, that would render the volume whole, total and coherent. But the base recedes before the advancing volume of experience, resisting completion. In the indeterminate darkness of the void, many pyramids interpenetrate and dissolve, one into others. They form a flux, a matrix of indeterminacy, an inconsistent pattern, a city of unknown origin and destiny, a politics not of being, but of becoming. Ontogenetics.

Social justice is not an issue of masses, but of individuals. If the mass is satisfied with its salutes, but an individual suffers, can there be justice — in human terms? To answer 'yes' is to justify oppression, for there are always people willing to lose themselves in a mass at the expense of some person who is not willing to do so. To construct a just society, it is precisely this lone person who must first receive justice. Call this person the inhabitant. Call this person *yourself*.

No one wants to discuss the relationship between architecture and politics. It is an unsavoury subject. All those politicians, all that rhetoric, mixed with the timeless verities embodied in the noble forms of architecture. Yet the resistance to enter this discussion is not noble at all. All architects are deeply involved in their work with the political, whether or not they admit it to others, or to themselves. Most architects in this highly commercial era, who accept commissions and clients that affect public life, are in fact committed to supporting the existing structure of authority as embodied in institutions of commerce and of its supporting political systems. Only a handful work against it, because they believe it is regressive in terms of architecture or society, or both. It is no wonder that the majority of architects avoid the political implications of their work. They believe themselves to be

8

creators, or innovators, when in actuality they are nothing more nor less than the executors of a physi-

cal and social order designed by those institutions presently holding political authority and power.

The practice of architecture today is protected from confrontation with changing political conditions

in the world within a hermetically sealed capsule of professionalism, which ostensibly exists to pro-

tect its high standards from the corrupting influence of political expediency and merely topical con-

cerns. Architects themselves are complicit with this lie to the extent that they know it is enforced by

the very institutions and individuals who commission the buildings they design, and who have a pro-

found economic and social interest in maintaining a *status quo* in which they hold highest authority.

Professionalism separates architects from people and their need to change the conditions of their

existence, which is the essence of all politics. Far from protecting the high standards of architecture,

this separation impoverishes architectural work, reducing its productions to tokens of power, at best,

and — at worst — to instruments of destruction.

The best architects today have few commissions, or none at all. Of course, they want to build, but are

dismissed by the institutions and individuals most threatened by the actual content of their work: an

explicit manifestation of the will to change the conditions of existence and the architectural means to

do it.

It is only recently that I have begun to speak and write about the essentially political nature of archi-

tecture, much to the disapproval of friends and colleagues who think the most worthy architecture is

above politics. I, too, would like to live in a time-capsule of 'unageing intellect', as Yeats wrote of his

beloved Byzantium. But — like him — I am unable to do so, and am compelled more and more to live and

work in the precise, often painful dimensions of the present. Since 1985, my projects have been a step-

by-step immersion into the world as it is — not as I, or Yeats, or anyone else who by nature is idealistic,

might wish it to be. With increasing decisiveness, these projects propose new social structures, imple-

mented by new urban forms and architectures, intended to be realised within existing cities. They are

inherently political, both in their rejection of existing social forms and proposal of new ones. The

vagueness of the new ones has been intentional, as they are essentially anarchical societies, lacking

in centralised political structure, centring instead on 'the individual' as the irreducible atom of commu-

nity and culture.

My work has developed and changed in the past ten years, precisely because change and develop-

ment of the forms of knowledge — and their effect on social and political structure — are its principal

themes at both the scale of the building and the scale of the city. In my projects for Four Cities of 1981-

82, AEON of 1983-84 and A City of 1985-86, Euclidian geometries were woven into rational two- and

three-dimensional matrices of cyclical — or recursive — transformations. I felt that a limit was reached

by the rational formalisms of these studies, which placed them, finally, too much in the realm of deterministic idealisation — they were incompatible with what became my own understanding of the non-deterministic nature of knowledge, and with it, the necessity of indeterminate anarchical social and political forms. In the Centricity project (1987), I introduced into a city of many centres — an already *anti-hierarchical* city — geometries of a more indeterminate nature, flowing from a hidden source of unpredictable change — call it 'the mystery of human inventiveness' — manifest in the always restless and unpredictable thoughts and desires and actions of individuals. In the projects that followed — Underground Berlin (1988), Aerial Paris (1989), Berlin-Free-Zone (1990), Zagreb-Free-Zone (1991), and Double Landscape, Vienna (1991) — this experiment was continued with one crucial, and obvious, difference: *actual* cities form the rationalised, over-determined matrix, while *free-zones* and *freespaces* — as I have come to call an architecture of indeterminacy — form the matrix of unpredict-able *possibilities* for cultural, social and political transformation latent in human knowledge and invention. In all these projects of the past ten years, there is an impulse towards a new comprehen-siveness, without the old necessity for a totality, a complete, predigested wholeness. These projects have the ambition to be a 'second nature', a fully realised, but deeply indeterminate human nature — a *terra nova*.

My emphasis on 'individuals' in the projects and my writing about them has left me open to criticism for being a right-wing thinker and architect, one who is not interested in issues of overall social justice or reform, but only in an elite who might occupy privileged positions of power and authority, by virtue of their self-serving ruthlessness, their solipsistic exercise of inventive faculties and capacities. I was shocked when this charge was made to me by a member of the audience at a symposium last year. But, to some extent, this is a just criticism, at least to the extent that *heterarchy* — the political form these anarchical projects seek to establish — can become the soil for authoritarian regimes, which are always cults of a particular personality. But I am against all authoritarian regimes, and against all authoritarians. I am interested only in the authority of individual acts and moments on a continually shifting landscape of acts and authority — the landscape of the *free-zone*.

On this landscape, no individual holds authority for long, because individual acts are ephemeral. There is, in this, an existential beauty, the type of beauty that cannot be grasped and held like a com-modity, in fact, beauty which does not pretend to be eternal and universal. On a landscape of ephem-eral beauty, no form and no individual holds authority for long, because no institution — political, social or cultural — exists to codify authority.

The role of architecture on this landscape is instrumental, not expressive. It is a tool extending individual capacities to do, to think, to know, to become, but also to pass away, to become an echo, a vestige, a soil for other acts, moments, individuals.

Existential beauty is destroyed by the impulse to possess, to own, to contain, to hold fast, therefore to dominate. Expression is possession, the manifestation of a lust for domination. Any attempt to express in a form an idea external to it is an attempt to arrest the idea in time, to control it beyond its life. I despise all such 'expressionism', and none more than that which appropriates ineffable symbols, archetypes — in fact, types of any kind. These are the most vain and tyrannical attempts to eternalise the ephemeral.

My emphasis on individuals focuses on their autonomy, which has meaning only within the context of *heteros* — an *other*. Dialogue is an essential aspect of heterarchy, as are other forms of interaction between people, and between people and things, such as buildings and spaces for living and work, such as the city itself. By contrast, in the hierarchical city — the city of the *hieros*, the holy — dialogue is always overshadowed by the monologues of authority, which issue from the apex of social and political pyramids of authority in the city and filter down, 'trickle down' (to borrow an infamous term of economics from the American Right) to the broad base of the city's life. In the hierarchical city, it is possible to imagine one simply 'being in it', utterly alienated from others — but in the heterarchical city, while one may choose to be isolated, the free flow of dialogue, unimpeded by monological authority, makes alienation unlikely. The difference between the hierarchical and the heterarchical city is the difference between *being* and *becoming*.

Dialogue precludes an entirely self-consistent system of thought or of architecture. Any such system is only monological, tautological, authoritarian, because it insists on belief above all else. Instead, I embrace systems admittedly incomplete, therefore tolerant of self-contradiction, self-paradox, self-reference, which — without dialogue — could not exist at all.

Heteros is the essence of the *free-zone* and *freespace* projects, hence also of dialogue and the politics that spring from it. These projects advocate the establishment of architectural activity that participates actively in dialogical political changes, assuming a role beyond that which architecture presently plays. It will not be enough for such an architecture to simply follow events and give them an appropriate architectural form. Rather, architecture must *initiate* events, even very aggressively foment them. The architect is not, in this case, a detached professional, upholding timeless values, but an instigator, an agitator, an active participant. One does not participate by following the crisis of change, but by being part of its initiation.

The architect's mandate for assuming such responsibility is, first of all, his or her mandate as a human being living in the contemporary world. The moral and ethical fabric of society has changed today from blind service to a hierarchy of authority, in whatever form, to a conscious personal responsibility for the condition of the world and others in it. Thus, the basis for making architecture has also definitely shifted. Today it is more ethical to actively propose new ways and conditions of living in which one can personally believe, than to represent by architectural or other means those ways and conditions the architect considers diminished or degraded, or those that change has clearly rendered outmoded and regressive.

It is not possible to cooperate with the present economic and political systems for the design and construction of architecture inherently opposed to any form of *status quo*. The relentless commercialism characteristic of these systems works against the realisation of an architecture initiating change in exactly the same ways as it does against change itself: by its appropriation as *a new status quo*. An architecture of the new must grow from a new conceptual ground, one having to do with the dramatic and sometimes violent changes that mark the present era. A new architecture for an era of radical changes in private and public life must actively participate in the establishment of new economic and political systems for the design and construction of buildings, and for the continued transformation of human communities around the world. This does not necessarily mean that the architect must propose a new society, though it might. At the least, it means that the architect must propose programmatic elements within a client's building programme, to account for qualities for which the architect, not the client, is responsible. It certainly means walking away from commissions to design types of buildings that neglect or subvert these qualities. More rarely, it may mean walking away from a practice of architecture altogether, in order to pursue personal research or experimentation.

My projects are concerned with the invention of new conditions of living. They are deeply political in nature, yet anti-ideological, in that they do not follow a programme for social relationships established *a priori*. Instead they develop an architecture of continuous transformation *for its own sake*, thereby undermining the very possibility of dogma in any form. Fixed social forms dissolve in the turbulences of change in the spatial and temporal boundaries established by architecture, projecting a society fluid in form, wholly dependent on the poise and ingenuity of individuals continually confronting new conditions. This fulfils the ethical and moral imperatives explicit in the sceptical, even pessimistic, spirit of the present age. Responsibility for the condition of both self and the world is fixed in each individual being. No system can be trusted. Any ideology is a betrayal. Only through the transformation of self can community be established. Architecture becomes a political act of intensely personal meaning.

Architecture as an instrument of transformation embraces with equal intensity of feeling and thought all conditions of physicality. It has no taste for the metaphysical, but is relentlessly materialistic. The visible and invisible are terms referring to bands on the electromagnetic spectrum. Thus the self-referentiality of transformation is established, the recursive loop between invention and perception given its mechanics. The comforts of tautology and solipsism are voided by dialogue: individual existence is confirmed only by and in an *other*. By establishing boundaries, an architecture of transformation demands their violation.

· As electronic technology extends perception of the invisible, the visible necessarily becomes more precious, more intense. The architecture of tactility cannot be separated from the architecture of ephemerality, either in concept or in implementation. Steel and the images on a computer screen are of the same material, perceived differently, each requiring the extremities inherent in their separate material presences. In my projects, architecture is an instrumentation of the tactile, seeking always the extremes of plasticity and variation, even as the instrumentation of the ephemeral penetrates more deeply into the very small, the very large, the very far, the very fast. The dialogical play of architecture and technology is inevitably epistemological and social, personal and political.

On a bright and clear day in July, 1987, I was driven to a *favela* in the Morumbi sector of Sao Paulo, Brazil. The labyrinth of shacks extended down a hill on the crest of which stood tall, white apartment houses, towers of the rich, commanding a valley of the poor. The newspaper and television reporters who took me there wondered what the reaction might be of a first-world architect to this local social diagram. It was late morning. The winter air was warm. We drove together down the hill on a rough dirt path that led into a small open space in the labyrinth. Children were playing in the dirt and sunshine, and a few teenagers stood about. They looked up as the car stopped and we got out, stepping into the ragged square. Their parents, I was told by the reporters, were away at jobs in the many busy factories of Sao Paulo, jobs that had drawn them to this place from the vast rural regions of Brazil. Because there was no housing for them, and no schools, and no medical care, they banded together, and built the *favelas*. The children stayed there during the day and into the night, waiting for the adults to return. Here there was no electricity, no running water, no sewage system to take away human waste or the water from storms that rake this hillside, washing away from time to time the more fragile parts of their fragile city. The small houses themselves were constructed of as many different materials as their builders could scavenge from the waste of the city — shards of wood, metal, cardboard, plastic, fastened tenuously together to form walls and roofs. I walked around for a few minutes, looking into one open house, then returned quickly to the dirt square. There a crowd of children had gathered, silently watching me. The reporters had taken a video camera from their car. One aimed it at me, while the other asked if I could please move a little to the right, so I could be framed against the shacks and the white towers above. I walked towards the car and told them we should go. As we climbed into the car, a few rocks smacked its side. The driver shoved it into gear and we rode up the rough path, the rocks and bottles picking up their tempo. As we reached the well-paved street above, the reporters asked me what architectural recommendations I would make to affect the conditions we had just seen. I answered, 'When you arrive at the scene of a human disaster, the first thing to do is stop the bleeding. There is nothing architecture can do until that is done.'

I was wrong.

COME THE REVOLUTION

A freespace structure was commissioned on June 16, 1991 by the Museum of Arts and Crafts in Zagreb, which is under the directorship of Professor Vladimir Malekovic. On June 26th, Croatia seceded from the Socialist Federal Republic of Yugoslavia, and was invaded by the Yugoslav Army. Since then, civil war has engulfed regions of Croatia. Much blood has been shed, much suffering has followed. Croatia's cultural fabric has been decimated, and its once-prosperous economy has been virtually destroyed.

What *is* this freespace structure, and the Free-Zone project of which it is a part, that they should be considered seriously in a context of violence, human suffering, even of despair over the aspect of humanity that so consciously imposes such conditions on people, in the name of 'national unity', or any other ideological premise?

The initial reception by the intellectual and arts community in Zagreb, and of the public, who became aware of the project through newspaper and magazine articles, was one of curiosity more than confirmation. To be sure, some of this curiosity centred on the fact that the architect was an American, from New York City. What does anyone from New York think of or care about Zagreb today? And why? Yet there is no doubt that curiosity also existed for reasons internal to the project presented entirely by drawings at the Museum of Arts and Crafts in April of 1991, reasons having to do with the very real and drastic changes then occurring, and about to occur, in the political and cultural life of the country. The idea of a series of mobile 'units of habitation' (occupied by whom was not clearly defined), packed with powerful communications and other advanced electronic instrumentation (also of unknown purpose), leaning against buildings, or suspended between them, occupying the streets of the city's centre like so many machines of war, could not help but provoke curiosity. Whether they were instruments of invasion, and, if so, to obtain what objectives, no one could say. Whether they were the refuges of gypsies intelligent and skilled enough to use the instrumentation, yet free in spirit enough to invent some purpose for its use not readily apparent, no one could say. Whether they are shelters for an elite who might seek to escape a coming storm of violence on a landscape about to be torn apart by war or social disorder, no one could say.

I asserted that the freespace structures and the constantly shifting pattern and network they created were 'heterarchical', and therefore an integral part of a global structure of freely determined communication and authority befitting a highly mobile and culturally dynamic contemporary urban society. Many questions raised by this assertion remain unanswered. Are the structures reserved for an elite of well-placed and well-connected intellectuals, artists, scientists, or — perhaps — for officials of the city, already invested with authority? Or are the structures inhabited by those aggressive and 'inventive' enough to seize and hold them — criminals and con men and renegades? Or are the structures meant for 'all individuals', which must include workers and farmers and fishermen? If so, then how will they possibly make use of the advanced instrumentation that is essential to the network, the ephemeral, McLuhanesque community on which this proposal depends?

It is not possible to name any individual or group as the designated inhabitants of the freespace structures and the free-zone network, without compromising its open nature and structure. At the same time, if inhabitation of the structure and the network is left open to whoever can 'seize' them, by whatever means, then the freedom of this aggressive elite could become a tyranny for others. Whoever occupies the freespaces and the free-zone will have control of the powers inherent in them: the power of access to global communications networks, with their databases and privileged information; the power to broadcast, and to interfere with the broadcasts of existing institutions of authority; the power to employ powerful electronic instruments extending the senses and capacities for experimental means; the power to move the structures freely within public space, for purposes no longer 'public' in the presently accepted sense of the word. If these powers are in the hands of egoistic inventors of self and world, then any *egalitarian* idea of human freedom is placed decisively at risk. There is no way to mitigate this risk. It is inherent in the inhabitation of freespaces and free-zones, unbounded as they are by any logic imposed by existing conventions.

The model of the heterarchical free-zone is a nucleic one — it begins with a small group of people, the inhabitants of the freespace structures. This group does not constitute a concentration of *institutionalised* authority — the freespace inhabitants have only the authority of their own performances. Their relationship to the city and its community depends solely on the quality of their interaction with them.

The free-zone is established on the principle of dialogue, carried on through instrumentation extending the senses and capacities of individuals into domains of the microscopic and macroscopic, facilitating direct experience of them. A type of instrumentation will be invented that facilitates *play* on the broad field of an individual's knowledge and experiences, a type of free interaction — a dialogue — with one's self that is in fact the beginning of all communication and community.

Freespace is a new spatial manifestation of the boundaries of individual autonomy. It is not interpreted by a social group in the form of a predetermined function or programme that is *named*, but only by an individual set of actions, purposes, meanings.

Freespace is not *demanded* by any of the existing cultural or social institutions, or even by an individual who has in mind for it some particular use. It does not belong to any existing building *type*, which excludes it from the marketplace. Instead it is constructed by an individual or small working group who see it in its inception as an instrument of transformation of 'self' and of 'world', by the very fact of its presence as a new, alien, indeterminate condition. Therefore it has definite possibilities — one might better say, *probabilities* (in the statistical, or quantum mechanical sense) — of implementation. Freespaces have no preconceived way of inhabitation. They are not goal-determined. Instead they are akin to experimental laboratories, with very precisely defined apparatus that can be used for a finite, but wide range of experimental uses. It is up to the inhabitant to determine, within the limits of the physical conditions of a particular freespace, how the freespace instrumentation — both architectural and electronic — will be used.

The range of probabilities of a given freespace's use is determined by the precisely defined configuration — the strong presence — of its spaces and forms. In inhabiting these, precision must be answered by precision, presence by presence.

The Cartesian grid so beloved of Modern architecture — and of Post-Modern architecture too — is not precise, rather it is a generalised abstraction. As a spatial and formal construct, it has no character, and therefore can be occupied without character, a fact to which many contemporary buildings testify. The dulling monotony of office work, and the general mediocrity of its results, for example, are not the *result* of the generalised neutrality of the Cartesian grid on which office buildings are based, but are *connected* symbiotically with it, on both conceptual and phenomenological levels.

Freespace, on the contrary, is quite precise spatially, dimensionally, materially. Its precision lies in the *differences* between one freespace structure and the next, between one space within that structure and the others, between one surface, texture, colour, degree of newness or decay, degree of lightness or darkness resulting from shifting conditions of illumination. Freespaces are not idealised abstractions, but concrete, existential realisations. To inhabit them, one must be equally concrete in one's thoughts and actions. It is not merely a matter of responding to the material characteristics, of reacting, but of a direct engagement, requiring an initiative, amplified, rendered forceful by a confrontation with 'useless' space. One has to invent something from almost nothing. In this case, the 'almost' — the precise existential conditions — is the crucial factor, and the crisis. Unlike the occupier of idealised space, the inhabitant of freespace must live poised in the precise material matrix of the present. Each freespace structure contains spaces that can be occupied by one or more persons. Occupation precedes inhabitation, and it will not be easy.

Freespace is 'useless and meaningless' space — space constructed with no predetermined use or meaning. On one hand, it appears that this is an unprecedented type of space, one that could only be seriously considered in Post-Modern conditions of a superfluity of goods and services — a kind of luxury of space. On the other hand, these Post-Modern conditions, as they have affected belief and value systems that once gave cohesion to society, make it clear that *all* spaces are useless and meaningless, until they are inhabited in specific ways. The Cartesian system for organising space has no more intrinsic usefulness or meaning than freespaces. The difference between these two has to do with their potential in the creation — through acts of inhabitation — of new values, purposes, uses, meanings.

In a sense, the conception and construction of freespace calls into question, or brings more into focus, the nature of constructed space generally, calling for a revaluation of existing cities and societies, as well as the 'use' and 'meaning' of any human life. My position is, however, not nihilistic. The assertion — through constructive action — of an intrinsic *emptiness* of human existence gives this emptiness value, which I refer to as a potential that an individual must realise through acts of inhabitation, acts of self-invention.

Self-invention inevitably draws upon and embraces the full scope of an individual's experiences. No one is born brand new each day, each moment. Much is drawn from conceptions of the past in the form of personal memories and reflections, as well as a social consensus about what the past was and meant — history and tradition. This, indeed, forms a framework for personal interpretations and interactions with the present, but not more than that. Today the burden of responsibility for inventing meaning and usefulness, through action, is on each individual, drawing as he or she might from all available resources. This is the essence — and the crisis — of the Post-Modern condition, the condition that informs the way people live on the anarchical landscape of emptied meaning and voided authority.

ATOMISATION

The global unification of nations seems well underway. Its basis is economic and financial. When the New York stock market crashed in 1988, a shockwave followed the sun, forcing steep declines in the London, Frankfurt, and Tokyo stock markets. This event destroyed the illusion that the world was divided into distinct nations and their respective cultures, and that human affairs — down to the level of the individual citizen of each nation — would continue to be decided in terms of national interests. It seems to be no coincidence that within three years of this event, socialism breathed its last in the countries of Central and Eastern Europe. No nation can now afford to miss out on the global unification game and hope to survive. The future will no longer be decided on the traditional competition between nation-states, but on the proficiency of international corporations and their loyal politicians in playing on a single financial field covering the entire planet, whose boundaries and markers are statistical, not geographical.

There is, however, another trend active in the world today, which opposes global unification and is therefore opposed by the institutions of finance and government promoting it. This is the trend towards a breaking of the nation-states into smaller and smaller units. Modern nations — such as the Soviet Union and Yugoslavia — have already broken up along historical and ethnic lines into smaller states. But these events will only be the initial phase of the atomisation of the planet.

If one traces the ethical development of Western civilisation, it clearly points towards the liberation of the individual from social masses. In the most advanced Western cultures, the evolution of political theory and systems, of education, techniques of transportation and communication, have already resulted in more autonomy for most individuals than has previously existed in its history. As this evolution continues in the West, and continues to spread itself into other cultures around the world, more individuals will achieve an unprecedented degree of mobility and choice, with all their existential benefits and burdens.

This second, anti-unification trend can be summarised in terms of politics, law, economics and culture: *the nation-state of the future is the individual human being*.

The individual human being is *organically* autonomous, in fact, an organism. Strictly speaking, a group of individuals is *not* an organism, however much philosophers and apologists of hierarchical structures might wish it to be, however much groups might behave *like* an organism in certain situations. *By nature, only the individual human being is autonomous*. When architects and planners speak of the city in terms of the human body — roads as 'arteries', communications networks as 'nerve systems', corporate and governmental headquarters as 'brain centres' — they make no more than a primitive analogy to the individual human organism, one that becomes tragic and totalitarian when CEOs and politicians, who wield power in society, act as though this analogy were literally true.

When I went to Brazil in 1987, I was taken to the top of the tallest building in Sao Paulo. There, as I teetered on a narrow catwalk, looking out in all directions over the city, the television people shoving their video cameras at me, asking what I would propose for their city of seventeen million inhabitants, I optimistically offered the results of my research up to that time. To solve the incredible congestion of traffic, to restore social equity, community and coherence to a mad landscape, the neighbourhoods should be reorganised according to the principles of Centricity. *'The universal science . . . whose workers include all individuals . . . seeks general principles whose discovery continuously reunifies all fields of knowledge on a universal plane, towards the achievement of an egalitarian and humanistic culture . . . The universal plane is the urban field.'* All those interlocking circles and cycles, like so many ripples on a smooth pond struck in the same instant by a handful of pebbles. A Leonardo drawing. A Renaissance ideal. The proper study of humankind is the human. Not so much a science of architecture, but science in the spirit of architecture.

From the height of the tower at the centre of Sao Paulo, the city stretched towards all horizons, confused, formless and uncontained. It was not universal, nor egalitarian, nor humanistic — a system too complex to see. An inconsistent pattern, lacking only a self-conscious architecture of insinuation, one that radically transforms and at the same time deeply preserves. Somewhere in the city, the life of the *favela* was eating away the roots of the serene white towers, a transformation their electronic surveillance systems would never detect. *Knowing a thing just as it is known.*

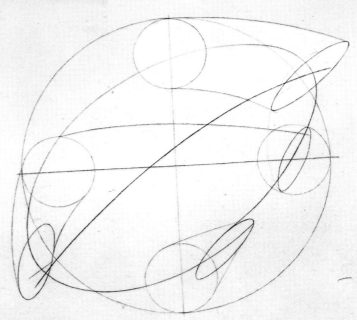

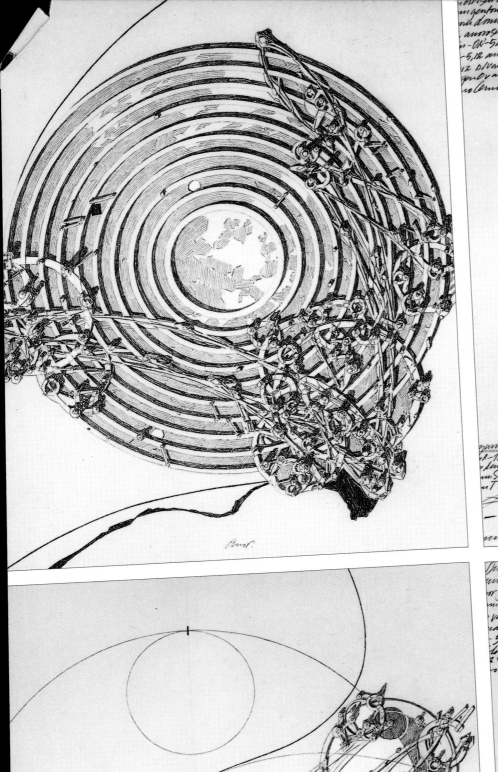

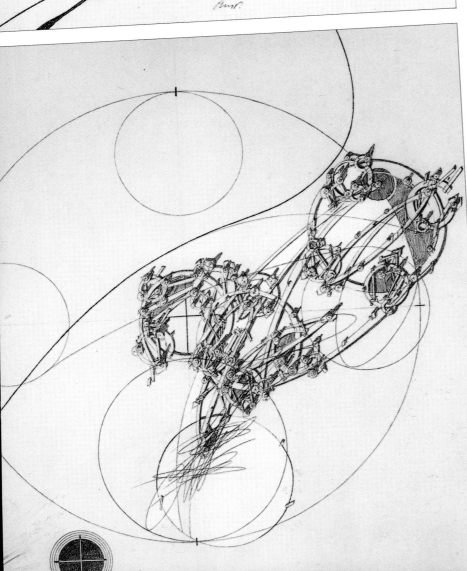

NEOMECHANICAL TOWER (UPPER) CHAMBER

Even for those who have never seen more than the little book on Centricity by Lebbeus Woods, the same conclusion remains: among all strange scenes of somebody else's domestic universe, embodied in towers, accumulators, livinglabs, fields and shafts, the strangest remains the picture of a small (upper) chamber of the neomechanical tower. Not that anything about the tower itself seems to be more comforting — 'comfort' is not the favourite word in Woods's personal thesaurus. Not that the fact of 'upper' evokes any vertigo — the chamber is one of those rooms without a view — the black-and-white version hides even the fact that an opening, bottom-left, leads to the abyss of a bluish vacuum. The upper chamber is one of the rare moments in this series of drawings depicting a notion of an inside, where one might have difficulties thinking of anything like an outside.

I suppose that this inability, or rather the fear of an imprisoned subject, made some viewers think that the upper is a chamber of torture. Torture would hardly lie in an elevated chair which seems to be dominating a bare landscape. Even the emptiness over which the chair, as any pointless dictator, governs all thinkable actions, is governed by another force stronger than three-dimensionals, by light which comes from the unknown source above it.

The difficulty with the upper chamber of the neogeomechanical tower hides in the very title of this piece, which, if read carefully, does not define the new geomechanical tower — the tower is old, as are the mechanisms. If one takes away, or tries to neglect 'romantic' notions — a deliberate love for decay, or irresistibly negligent, therefore modern, evidence of indifference — it makes it easier to think that, as in some of the best verses of English poetry, 'time present and time past are both present in time future'; that the drawing grew old in the process of its making, in order to speed up the time of actual awaiting. What is new in this story is the earth, the world — a so-called 'celestial body where humans live' — any idea of land, state, notion of property, and therefore of society and civilisation. For those who want to ask questions which are not sterilised in advance by normatives of modern, post, contemporary, actual — there remains the rare chance to ask whether it is possible to think of the creation of spaces which demands a different point of departure than 'moving in'. The upper chamber — as all other space-proposals of Woods's *universum* — cannot be ornamented by previous 'belongings'; it cannot be adopted through the performance of old actions. It demands its own civilisation of living, which probably answers the ultimate question: Why is it empty?

Aleksandra Wagner

CENTRICITY IS AN ADJECTIVE AND A NOUN, THE MODIFIER AND MODIFIED. New patterns of urban form and living arise from concepts of time and space considered as one, as *timespace*. The interplay of metrical systems establishing boundaries of material and energetic form is the foundation of a universal science (*universcience)* whose workers include all individuals, whose principle instrument of research is architecture, and whose interactive field is CENTRICITY.

THE AIM OF RESEARCH IS KNOWLEDGE, AND THAT OF KNOWLEDGE, ACHIEVEMENT. A universal science seeks general principles whose discovery *continuously* reunifies all fields of knowledge on a universal plane, towards the achievement of an egalitarian and humanistic *culture* of universality. This universal plane is the *urban field*, universally experienced and within which the timespace continuum is universally perceived and understood.

THE ROOTS OF A UNIVERSAL SCIENCE EXIST WITHIN PRESENT KNOWLEDGE. Visible light is the wave-phenomenon constant to matter and energy (*mattergy*) in the universally perceived urban field. Visible light is *formed* by architecture that reveals an intrinsic order, that is, a form of visible light's metrical transformations. The architectonic mathematics (*archimatics*) of visible light is the foundation of the general principles of a universal science. *The*

architecture and urban forms of a *universal science* reveal the *timespace transformations of metrical light* (*cf* Le Corbusier's 'Architecture is the masterly, correct and magnificent play of forms assembled under light.')

A CENTRICITY OF UNIVERSAL SCIENCE EXISTS WITHIN THE PRESENT TIMESPACE-OVERTAKEN. An architecture of dynamism (geodynamism, biodynamism, mechanodynamism) moves recursively towards order and disorder as unity, and is composed of dual metricalities (geometric, biometric, mechanometric) of unified timespace: the centrisymmetrical and eccentrisymmetrical (circular and elliptical), corresponding respectively to quadrupolar (QUAD) and deformed-quadrupolar (D-QUAD) timespace rings, according to visible light distribution and Relativistic distortions.

THERE IS NOTHING TO CREATE BUT VISION. Visual research yields a unification of reductive knowledge into expansive knowledge sought by a universal science. The visible urban field continuously reunified by vision of metrical light is timespace recursively overtaken by itself. The resulting knowledge-sphere (*epistesphere*) is small, but powerfully concentrated by centricity. Yet centricity also impels timespace expansion to the limits of the visible universe and beyond, to the anti-limits of timespace invisibility: the

Freefield. There the unknown is but the unenvisioned form of metrical light.

THERE IS BEAUTY OF FORM ONLY WHERE THERE IS BEAUTY OF IDEA. (June, 1987)

The cycles are not empty now, it is simply that from within them, their whole form is visible only at certain times. This is not one of those times. Now one can perceive only the present phase of the cycle — any sense of the whole is lost. Cycles within cycles. God, how I laboured in that field, for years trying to reconcile determinism with doubt. Architecture seemed the perfect ground on which such a metaphysical knot could be untied — by the method of Alexander of Macedon. No puzzling, no arguments, just pure experience. Knowing a thing just *as* it is known. No dualisms or those other tight systems that end in resolution, therefore in spiritual death. Better to know nothing, than to know those as true.

Centricity. Both a quality and a thing, present in a place. A city of many centres, an unpredictable number of centres, overlapping, interpenetrating one another. Interfering with one another. Annoying, disturbing, in conflict, one atom with the next. Or amplifying one another, building energies together that none could attain alone. A hypothetical city, held together by 'laws' — the universal structure of the cycles — unpredictable in form and the infinite

possible variations on law and universal structures. Like so many individual beings — each human, yet different. The only basis for community.

The numerous plans (which may be seen as simultaneous or consecutive) are dualistic. Static Euclidean shapes are invaded by some other more dynamic geometry, the figures of which seem random, but are not, because they are the product of design. The static figures are hierarchical, deterministic; the dynamic figures are dominated by a metrical system based on a heterarchy, or unpredicted and indeterminate network, of discrete centres, from which radiate the activities of individuals and communal groups, coalesced in the forms of architectural construction. The dominant plan form is the circle circumscribing each centre to a degree and scope corresponding with each centre's activities. The interaction of activities among the separate centres results in the overlaying and penetration of the organising circular constructions. Almost nowhere is the circular form closed, inviolate, complete.

This condition is consistent with a concept of time described by the circle: the timecycle. Much of the physical world manifests its dynamic structure of the growth and decay in cyclical terms, the forms of which are derived from symmetries fundamental to nature's intricate fabric of light, energy and matter.

The overlaying and complexity of cyclical, circular forms demonstrate the inherent power of symmetry to assert its presence, even though the form it inhabits is interrupted and fragmentary. The centricity plan is an accumulation of symmetries, a webbing of cycles intersecting in space and time.

Each cyclical form refers to an idealised four-part substructure, a *quadrupolar* form, perfectly balanced about two axes of symmetry normal to one another, comprising opposing halves and quarters. A double complementarity results from any specific orientation in time and space, relative to fixed and moving points of light. In its idealised state, the quadrupolar form reveals the precise light-metrical fabric of time and space. The quadrupolar is an instrument for the apprehension of fundamental light, energy and matter relationships and the dynamic of their equivalence.

In their fragmentary state, the quadrupolar forms of centricity reveal that the fabric of the physical world only roughly corresponds to any idealisation, and in fact is not comprised of ideal symmetries, but of symmetries broken by the dynamism of this equivalence. A continual transformation of energy to matter and matter to energy is mediated by visible light and other electromagnetic wave phenomena. The quadrupolar forms of centricity are distorted by a dynamism of growth and decay, of construction and its inevitable succumbing to the ravages of entropy. As each cycle of construction ends, some portion of its quadrupolar structure remains, a vestige that influences to some degree future developments of the urban form.

From a viewing point on the groundplane, the cyclical quadrupolar forms of centricity are less apparent, but subtly present. In the fully developed three-dimensional structures that occupy the quadrupolar rings of construction, the centripetal and centrifugal effects of activities about their loci are manifest in vertical axes and multiple, broken symmetries.

Each complex of structures, rising from a quadrupolar ring, is a compact neighbourhood in which a community of individuals work and live. The interpenetration of separate structures, as of the rings themselves, reveals the complexity of any transformation, but most especially that resulting from continuous human interaction. Goods and services are exchanged. Communication is carried on. Yet the architecture reveals another, deeper interaction of centricity's inhabitants with one another, and with the wider world.

The architecture of centricity, independent of purely material necessity, plays with light, its symmetries and breaking of symmetries, its shifts and intricate interweavings. The structures are instruments of play. At the same time, they are instruments of physical knowledge, or — perhaps more accurately — a knowledge of physicality. The structures, organised by interrelated and sometimes conflicting symmetries, are of permanent construction, yet they are overlaid with more transitory tectonic elements — examining machines. The towers are in effect axial armatures around which turn activities requiring the making of instruments increasing human sensitivity to the continual flux of the physical: oscilloscopes, refractors, seismometers, interferometers, telescopes, microscopes. Also there are instruments of as yet undefined purpose, that can only be defined generally, measuring and manipulating light, movement, force, change. Tools for extending human capacity are built spontaneously, playfully, experimentally, and are continuously modified in home laboratories, or — more accurately — in laboratories that are homes. The structures are *laboratories for living*. Founded on idealised forms and principles, the structures are changed throughout the cyclical evolution of their construction. They are transitory, tentative, transitional — as experimental as the living within.

Living experimentally means *living continuously at the limit of received knowledge*. An individual and a community sustain experiments in living by being both skilful and playful, by mastering much knowledge of physicality and physical skills, yet at the same time going beyond them to acquire knowledge and skills not known before, nor predicted by knowledge already held. In centricity,

this paradoxical state of both being and becoming (in strictly phenomenological terms) is attained through continuous engagement with the light-metrical fabric of the physical world, and increasingly through instrumentation: architectonic, electronic, and mechanical — the playful examining machines.

Centricity is a city in which architecture is not merely a background for living, a pragmatic convenience, and even less a luxury afforded by the few; rather, it is an active part of the knowing and doing of each inhabitant, nothing less than a medium for living founded on physical knowledge and knowledge of the physical.

At this stage in the development of liberal democracy, the emergence of all individuals from the undifferentiated background of nature and of mass culture seems at once imminent and unlikely. All the necessary intellectual and technological tools are at hand, yet the ethical and political will to assemble them into a physical construct facilitating emergence — a new *type* of city — has not been made, but is thwarted by ancient and self-destructive forces still active in individuals and their society.

In the present technological society, innovation has already begun to race ahead of tradition. Technology cannot become a tradition. New knowledge, new conditions of living are developing faster than can be thoroughly assessed and tested, or their effects

controlled. These conditions force changes in thinking and society, from which a new coherence — and new *type* of coherence — must come.

Practitioners of architecture, who see it as an active form of knowledge, can consciously play a greater role in the accelerated processes of transformation than those who do not and give in quite readily to the demands of purely commercial interests. Most architects today seem confused when they confront new technology, knowledge and conditions of living, preferring either to ignore them or fall back on stereotypes. Their confusion will end only when architects accept that the mandate for practising architecture today is not the control of change, but its *invention*.

NEOMECHANICAL TOWER (UPPER) CHAMBER

I am standing now outside the drawing, an onlooker. Once I was inside, on the other side of the paper's surface. Then, in the space and time of the drawing's making, I moved with such ease back and forth through the now impenetrable barrier, the boundary between seeing and making — I remember that. I moved so easily in the space between the mind and the hand, between the eye the extension of the hand pressed into the paper's surface. The evidence of the pencil's entry into the paper, to the paper's inside, are the marks that trace outlines and surfaces of a different order. The tower chamber.

Two chambers, really. From inside the first a second can be seen. Beyond that, the sky. A table can be seen in the second chamber, two chairs, a carpet — or pattern — on the floor. On the table is a bowl. Food is about to be served, or has already been. Whoever will eat there will not, or does not, want to eat alone. Also there will be a view, some fresh air. A natural landscape lies beyond, trees, forests, fields, rivers roll out under an azure sky. It is summer, late spring, early autumn — the window is open and there is a terrace onto which those who have had their meal can move later to take in the air and view. Or there is a cityscape beyond, I can't be sure. The room is too high above the ground to tell. A cityscape rolling dark and clamorous out under a sky that is blue, but vaguely sinister in the opacity of its blueness. I find it a disquieting blue, thick with a greyness having nothing to do with the crystalline lightness of summer skies, or the transparency, the infinity of spring and autumn. It is winter, or close to it. I see now that the balcony has no guardrail — too dangerous to go out there. And the window has no frame, no glass at all. It's chilly in the second chamber, if winter is coming on. The table is bare. The chairs are empty.

But the first chamber, into which the onlooker sees through the drawing's hard square of frame, is a different matter. No connection to the world outside is visible, or implied. I cannot *sense* a connection — none seems necessary. One enters, or leaves, this

chamber through another hard square of frame (why do I know it's square?) — a doorway to the second chamber. There is no other way. Only one wall is visible — the wall on which the chair is mounted — and its height is truncated by the drawing's frame. The wall to the left, with the doorway, and the wall to the right is solid, unbroken. The wall that lies behind must be unbroken — the chamber is too concentrated, too isolated, withdrawn from any world outside its walls to allow more than a single opening to violate its *sanctum*. The only light falling into the chamber is from above, and it flows downward on the walls, revealing their heavy textures, their contrasting patterns of strict geometry and random decay. The walls seem neglected, for want of care, or indifference to the peeling away over time of numerous finishing layers concealing the interior of the walls' construction. It seems possible that the neglect is intentional. Possible because each object in the chamber — chair, the rails on which it can be moved, the heavy cables suspended to the chair or coiled loosely on the floor, and the instrument suspended from the wall, approaching the chair as if to address it — all these things seem deliberately placed, fully intentional. This is no ruin. No litter lies about to distract from the purposefulness of the space. The peeling of the surface of the walls is intended to reveal deeper-lying layers of material, to force a new geometry over the familiar and deterministic geometry of the

walls' design. The randomness of entropy and the indifference of destruction overlaying the predictability of designed construction. A time limit, a *memento mori*, a conscious release of control. Intellect acknowledging, even celebrating, its limitations. Mind's flirtation with the body's death. Mind's courtship, therefore, with its own.

TURBULENCE

Architecture that arises from and sinks back into fluidity, into the turbulence of a continually changing matrix of conditions, into an eternal, ceaseless flux — architecture drawing its sinews from webbings of shifting force, from patterns of unpredictable movement, from changes of mind, alterations of position, spontaneous disintegrations and syntheses — architecture resisting change, even as it flows from it, struggling to crystallise and be eternal, even as it is broken and scattered — architecture seeking nobility of presence, yet possessed of the knowledge that only the incomplete can claim nobility in a world of the gratuitous, the packaged, the promoted and the already sold — architecture seeking nobility of persistence in a world of the eternally perishing, itself giving way to the necessity of its moment — architecture writhing, twisting, rising and pinioned to the unpredictable moment, but not martyred, or sentimental, or pathetic, the coldness of its surfaces resisting all comfort and warmth — architecture that moves, slowly or quickly, delicately or violently, resisting the false assurance of stability and its death — architecture that comforts, but only those who ask for no comfort — architecture of gypsies, who are hounded from place to place, because they have no home — architecture of circuses, transient and unknown, but for the day and the night of their departure — architecture of migrants, fleeing the advent of night's bitter hunger — architecture of a philosophy of interference, the forms of which are infinitely varied, a vocabulary of words spoken only once, then forgotten — architecture bending and twisting, in continual struggle against gravity, against time, against, against, against — barbaric architecture, rough and insolent in its vitality and pride — sinuous architecture, winding endlessly on and through a scaffolding of reasons — architecture caught in sudden light, then broken in the continuum of darknesses — heroic architecture, that always reaches for more than it can grasp, possessed of the wisdom that there are no more heroes — heroic architecture, the forms of which are modest, never showing too much of the hidden sources of their strength — architecture embracing the sudden shifts of its too-delicate forms, therefore indifferent to its destruction — architecture which destroys, but only with the coldness of profound respect — neglected architecture, insisting that its own beauty is deeper yet — abandoned architecture, not waiting to be filled, but serene in its transcendence — architecture that transmits the feel of movements and shifts, resonating with every force applied to it, because it both resists and gives way — architecture that moves, the better to gain its poise — architecture that insults politicians, because they cannot claim it as their own — architecture whose forms and spaces are the causes of rebellion, against them, against the world that brought them into being — architecture drawn as though it were already built — architecture built as though it had never been drawn —

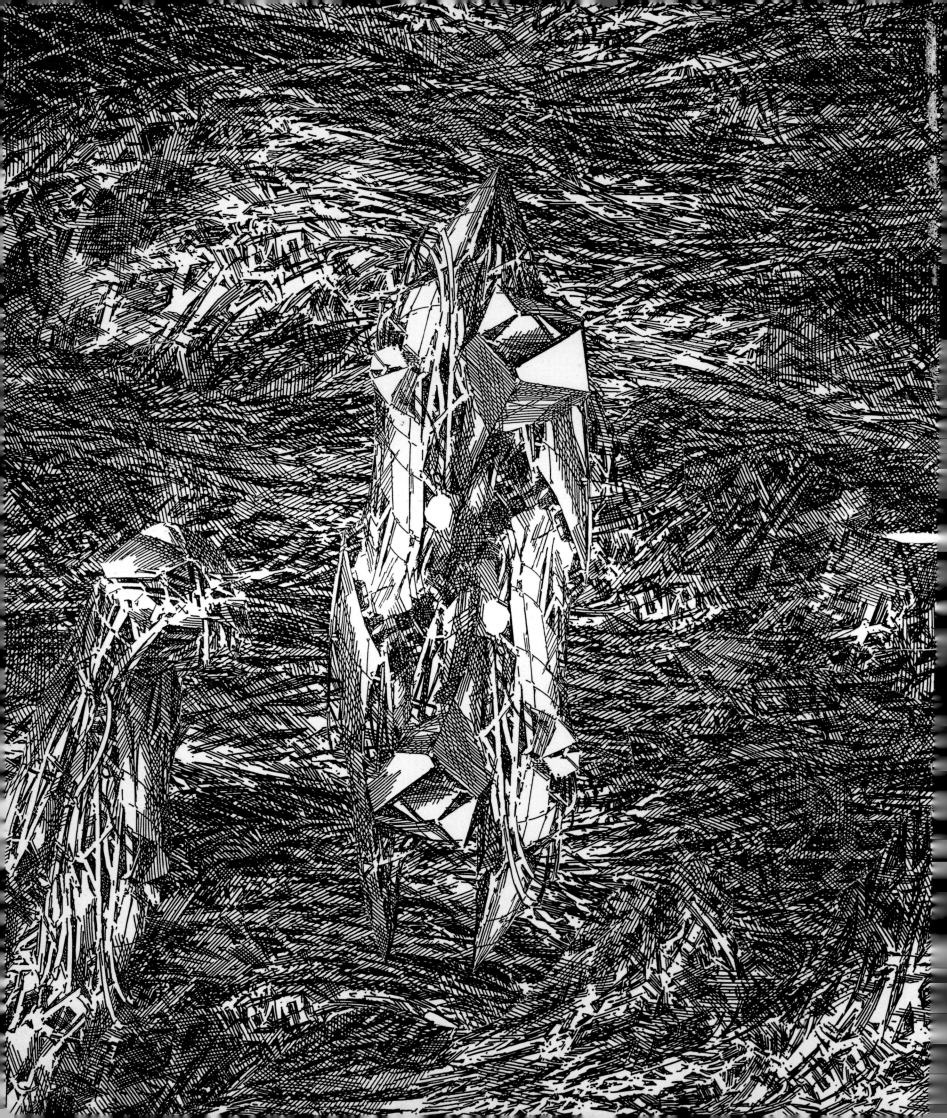

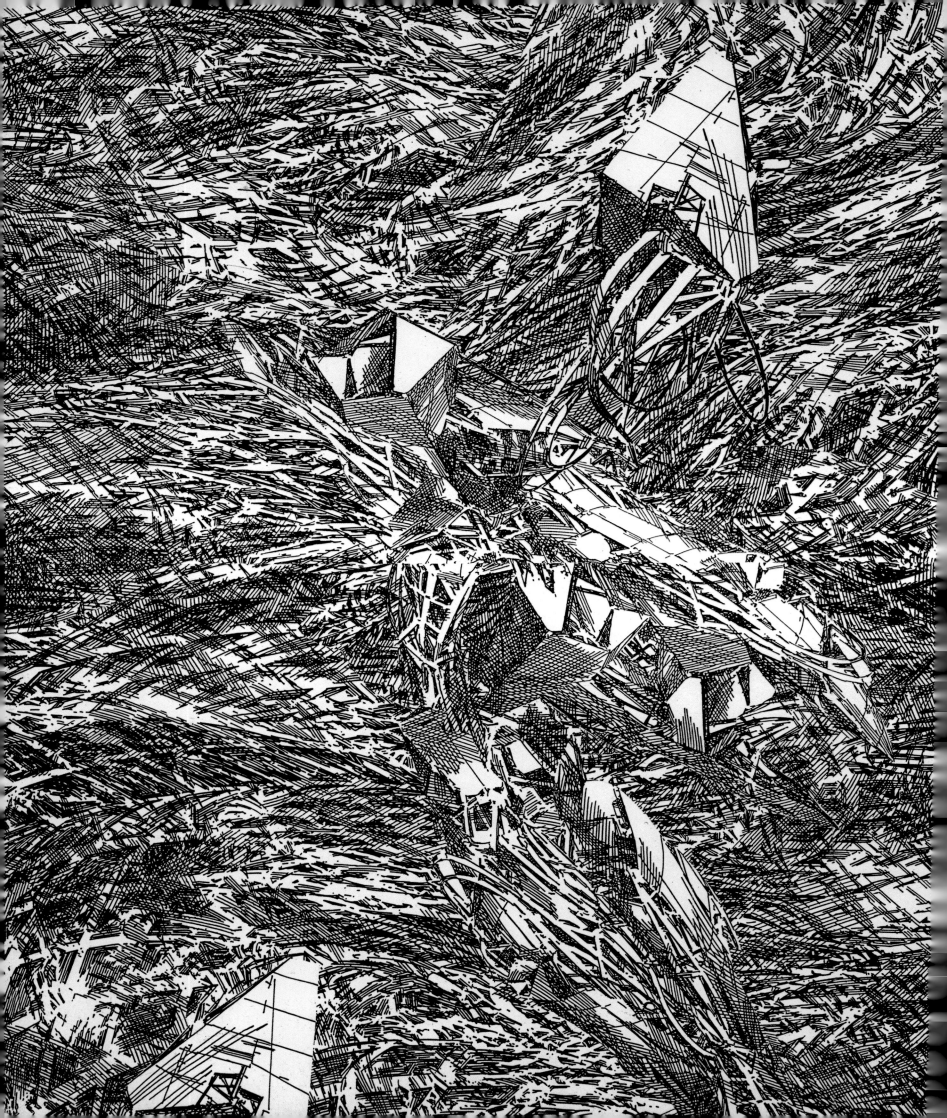

HETERARCHIES

So long as the concept of hierarchy dominates architecture (as it presently does), architecture will stay rooted in classical models, at the urban and building scales alike. So long as architecture stays rooted in classical models (as it presently does), it will continue to express an old, even archaic, idea of knowledge. So long as architecture expresses another idea of knowledge than that which best serves the present conditions of living (as it presently does), architecture will be a regressive force in the world of human affairs, even of human existence itself.

The archaic form of knowledge is that defined by Aristotelian rules of logical classification. There are three laws of logic, according to Aristotle, three figures in the Trinity, according to Christian doctrine, three laws of planetary motion, according to Kepler, three aspects of the psyche, according to Freud. More to the point, there are three straight sides to a triangle — the most stable geometric form — according to Euclid, and a triangular basis to the pyramid, the archetype of all hierarchical architecture, because it is the most perfect hierarchical form. In the pyramid, the apex dominates the base, no matter how large the pyramid, no matter how broad the base. Authority, whether of an intellectual, spiritual or political kind, is invested in this apex, and may be said to flow downward, by a kind of gravity, from it — when it flows at all.

This is neither a game of numbers nor of words, but an insight into a system of thought, an idea of knowledge, and an apparatus of social and political organisation which has long provided Western civilisation with an equilibrium for its activities and history, its understanding and, therefore, its progress. This is a system, an idea and an apparatus that succeeded so long because of its immense practicality. The Law of the Excluded Middle is as expedient to the scientist as the triangle is convenient to the carpenter, and the organisation chart is to the bureaucrat. That hasn't changed, nor is it likely to. What *has* changed is the nature of the equilibrium required by contemporary culture, for which the very concept of knowledge, rooted in some system of logic, must serve in various ways.

Self-preserving cultures seek static equilibrium, the maintenance of a *status quo*, as the founding principle of social coherence. The means of this maintenance is conformity to standards and norms. Contradictions, conflicts and paradoxes are intolerable in such societies, because they are inconsistencies that undermine requisite conventions.

Contemporary society is not self-preserving, but essentially *self-transforming*. It seeks dynamic equilibrium. Continual change is what it is based on, and what it needs above all else. This extends fully into the realm of knowledge, what it is and what it means today. Knowledge is no longer that inertial body of facts which enforces stasis, but is in fact the impetus to and energy driving change on every level of society and culture. Dynamical social coherence is possible — paradoxically, in Aristotelian terms — only within an *incohering* field of knowledge, and therefore of action, a continually shifting and self-transforming field, within which the constituent parts retain a certain autonomy, freedom of expansion or of instant annihilation, and are not subjected to totalising systems of any kind.

The idea to construct a subterranean community along lines of the U-Bahn beneath the centre of Berlin originated with the desire to undermine — physically and ideologically — the Wall dividing East and West Berlin, as an active move by Berliners themselves towards the reunification of their city and culture. Since the time of the project's inception the unification of Berlin and Germany has been accomplished, and by quite different means.

In this project the subversion of an existing authoritarian system of social control is accomplished by architectural means. Subversion by constructive means immediately becomes an affirmation, even though of an as yet undefined order replacing the one subverted, avoiding the dilemma of nihilism. The construction of a new city within and in opposition to an existing one amounts to an act of renunciation and even of violence, more lasting in its effects than those achieved by the gun. One need only compare the changes made to cities by modern war and by modern architecture to confirm this idea. The process of changing from one type of order to another is always violent. Over time, architecture can be the most potent weapon of change.

The architectural means of subversion proposed in this project begin with the occupation of territory in the city that has been previously neglected, abandoned or ignored by existing institutions of authority, both public and private. In this project, this is the space in the earth beneath Berlin. The construction there of spaces for communal and private life undermines the authoritarian structure above, but at the same time affirms an entirely new set of living conditions, those resulting from the physical climate of forces — geomechanical and geomagnetic — active within the planetary mass of the earth.

From these new conditions comes this project's non-hierarchical urban form, a linear network of autonomous living and working structures that interact with the earth forces in ways possible only within the mass of the earth: resistantly, dissonantly, but always with a direct engagement that is comparable with the ways the architecture of the surface city interacts with the forces of the atmosphere into which it projects, the climate formed by the forces of air and wind, of sun and the moon. The architecture of a subterranean world interacts with extremely subtle electrical and seismic fields, the basis of an equally subtle and experimental way of living. The light and loosely-knit metal construction of the network of living and working spaces and the structures — the living-laboratories — enables their interaction, singly and as a heterarchical urban unit, with the precise, but mathematically indeterminate complexities of the earth's inner climate.

The principal difference between the way of living underground and that of the existing city above is the difference between inner and outer, depth and surface. Above, the city exists on the frictional plane where earth and sky abrade one another, a condition of boundary, which is in many ways two-dimensional. The groundplane is dominant, and the groundplan the principal generator of architecture. Below, within the mass of the earth, no referential plane equivalent in power, authority and influence exists to flatten the dimension of human activity and perception into primarily two dimensions. Here a fuller plasticity of thought is not only possible but demanded, and with it a three-dimensional architecture that is instrumental in extending experience fully into space.

A certain irony is apparent here. Space is spoken of where only mass exists. The three-dimensionality of the underground exists as a fact, but actual spaces of human habitation must be created — the voids to be filled by human movement and activity. Herein lies another essential difference between life below and above: the sensibility of carving, of subtraction as the basis of making space, as opposed to the modelling, the building up of space. The carver is more deliberate, slow and silent. It takes more energy to carve. Once removed, the carved mass cannot be replaced.

The civic space of the underground community is filled by people and their activities, but also by their modelled instruments of living, the technological extensions of their existence implementing a way of living different from that of the city above. Architecture is principal among these.

The tectonics of the underground structures for living and work first of all, attunes them to the particular climate of geomagnetic and geophysical forces ambient in the planetary mass of the earth. Through this connection, then, it is possible to assert a human presence within the already animate existence of the earth, creating a recursive relationship between the artificial and the natural, a feedback mechanism completing a cycle of exchange between the human and extra-human. Architecture in this case is not only an instrument for receiving and passively controlling the forces of environment (the aim of any architecture), but also an instrument of transmitting energy, in effect relinquishing control to the environment, but in the process gaining a more powerful reciprocation with it.

The hierarchical surface city is met by the heterarchical subterranean city in structures built to break the physical and ideological barrier between them. The projection towers are architectural weapons *par excellence*. They have every intention of disrupting, of tearing the fabric of the surface city and its way of life. Staging towers for the construction of kinetic,

germinal elements embodying the political and cultural energies of Underground Berlin, they are instruments of a wider transformation to come.

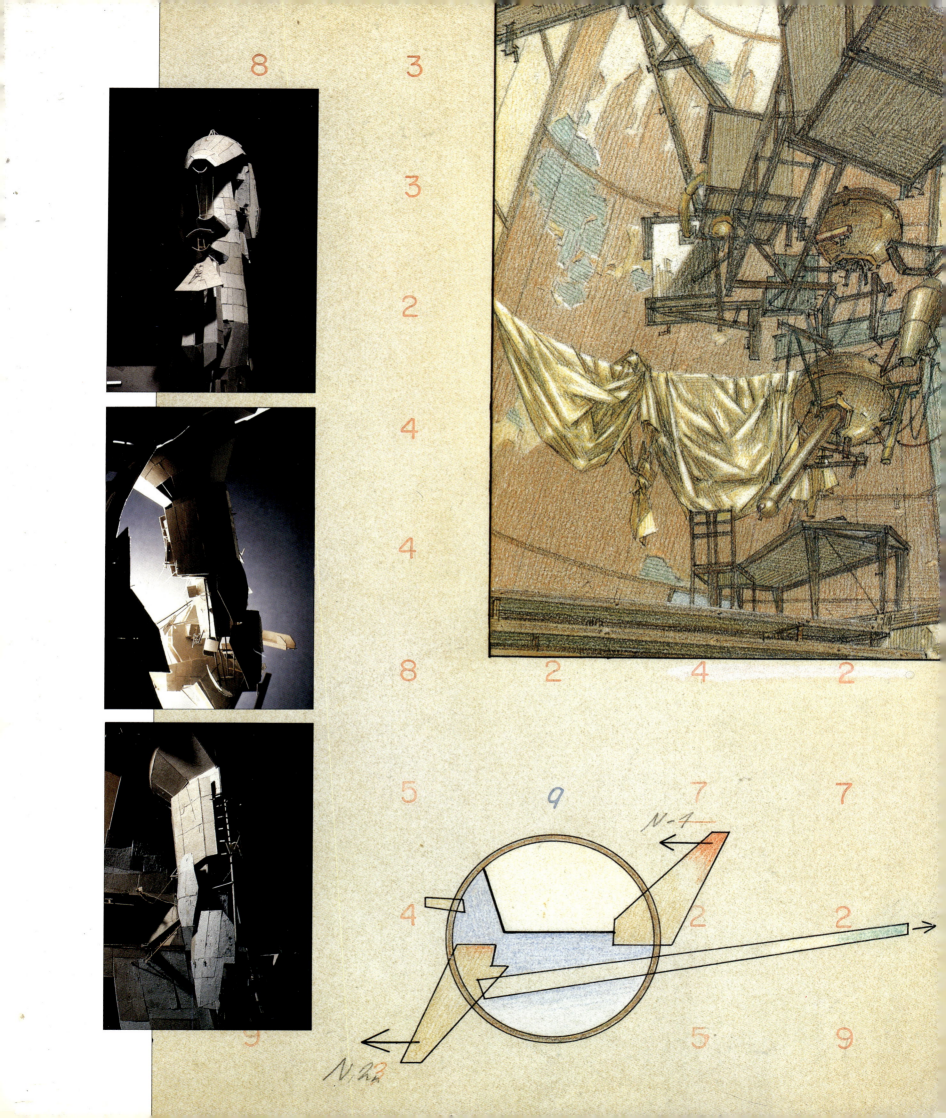

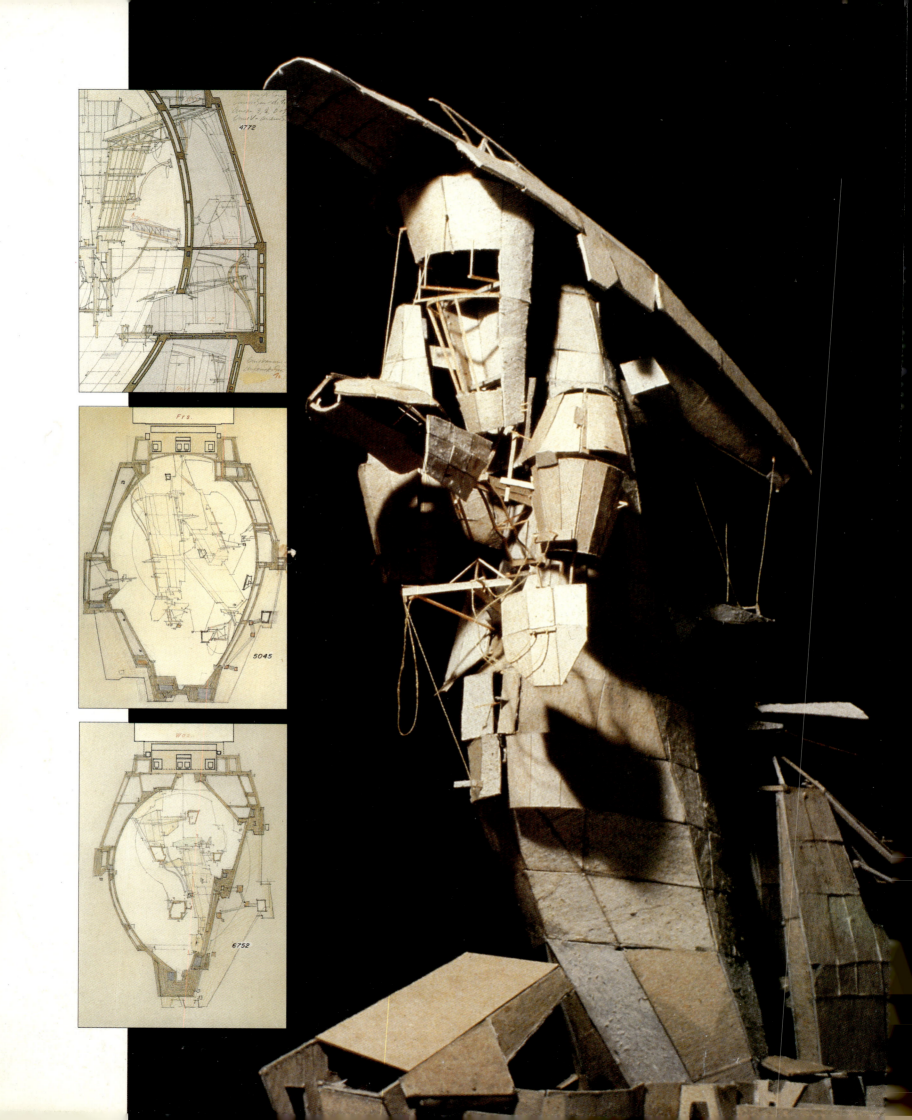

7

9 3 8 2

7 6 0 0

8 5 7

g

1 0 2

2 9 3 9 5

Antigravity refers to struggle, tension, anxiety and a restless assertion of the kinetic and animate against stasis.

Gravity is an insidious enemy of the animate. It is ever-present on earth, and is forgotten, or — like a member of the family — seems constant, reassuring, benign. But it continuously drains the energies of living, animate things, as they struggle against it, in order to move, to live. The struggle against gravity wears out the living, and eventually claims them, drawing them down forever into the earth, gravity's massive source.

I therefore declare myself against gravity, because I am for animation and movement. And I choose to declare war on gravity and proclaim it an enemy who, though possessed of a certain nobility, arrogantly claims control over my existence. I reject gravity's arrogance and claims, and assert a counterclaim — I am a free spirit, autonomous and self-determining, a being and an architect of antigravity.

If I could believe in utopia, it would be a utopia of free movement, a perpetual assertion of self-determined existence in space and time. But I cannot believe in utopia, so I believe in movement attained through and limited by struggle, tension, anxiety and the assertion of my personal power against the power of the earth, against gravity and death.

I cannot believe in utopia, because utopia insists on an absolute consensus among people, and

such a consensus cancels the individual's power to assert his and her presence in the world. Consensus is an ally of gravity. It is in fact a form of gravity that slowly and insidiously disables individuals and makes them impotent before the relentless claims of gravity and death. I declare war on consensus.

Experimental architecture is not an architecture of consensus, but of individuals lonely and angry enough, cold and passionate enough to assert themselves without the sanction of others, and in this way come into a human interaction with the world. Struggle, tension, anxiety and a restless assertion of the kinetic and animate against all forms of and tendencies towards stasis — these are ingredients of the human presence on and against the earth.

The aerial houses of my project for Paris are in a physical sense like the individuals who inhabit them: extremely expansive and three-dimensional, striving always for plasticity, freedom of movement and a continuous victory over gravity. The houses' composite forms combine diverse elements in order to attenuate sensations and perceptions of light, space, air. Their visual aspects are of primary importance, because seeing is primary to the inhabitants of these aerial structures. But one might well imagine, too, the sounds of wind upon and within their metal shells, and the touch of unyielding materials, vibrat-

ing as they do in their movement through ethereal streams of air. As for the more esoteric and intimate senses, what might the fragrance be of air at 3,000 metres above Paris, or the taste of the wind?

To attenuate sensation is to attenuate time — most specifically, the time of the present. 'Past' and 'future' are remote abstractions compared to the immediacy of the present, perhaps useful in a life made up of abstractions, but of mere practical value in aerial existence: precision in the measure of space and time fixed as mere coordinates. What is vivid and actual is the glint of sunlight on metal, the sudden drop felt in the pit of the stomach when falling, the irregular beat of one loose cable on another. What is vivid and actual is the word just now being spoken, the movement just being made or felt. The concepts of past and future are valuable only to the degree that they become or remain of the vivid present, the actual *becoming* of a moment. Past and future are to be considered, but only in order to be forgotten in the presence of experience.

The aerial structures above Paris are not designed — they are made. Design invokes the future — it prescribes something that will happen, hoping to control it. Making is in the present. Metal is fastened to metal. Paint is applied to wood. Making is happening now. Ideas of controlling overall form, ideas of wholeness and totality are only vestiges of old fears, terrestrial fears. The ambiguity of becoming strikes fear in the earthbound. For them the idea of being offers security, identity, fixity, all the illusory comforts of the controlled, the known-in-advance, the predicted, the designed. But the domain of the skies is too complex in its currents and countercurrents, too transitory in its invisible fluidity, too uncertain in its potentials for all but those who value most the delicacy and severity of a single act of poise, a balancing act sustained for just this moment between the abysses of before and after. The aerial house, the aerial community, metal, glass, wood, wire — all give the possibility of striking a balance, but not its assurance. The inhabitants of Aerial Paris are performers in a circus of becoming, without hope of arriving even once at a place in time where they have already been.

The unrepeatability of house forms — or even of the permutations of a single house's form — is inevitable. Nothing is 'ever again' what it once 'was'. Things only 'are', vivid and actual only as they are, in the abbreviated or attenuated present.

The aerial houses are not examples of generic types, much less of Platonic ideas. They cannot be described except in specific terms: *the aerial box, 12.46 metres high, 8.9 metres deep . . . with projecting copper forms . . . with a hairline crack in the third panel from the bottom-left . . . with the sun (from behind high, thin clouds) 47 degrees 42 minutes from the horizon . . .*

The inhabitants of the aerial houses have names, but these do not refer to past-future continuities or identities; rather they are expressions of affection, curiosity, disgust, delight.

To the earthbound, these aspects of aerial existence seem absurd. But then, the circus is absurd, a collection of meaningless acts of amusement over living and dying within the same moment. This present moment, too, is absurd, ceasing to exist in the very instant of its birth. The earthbound and aerially-bound are absurd, dying even as they live, the difference between them being that the former do not know it and the latter do not care.

From below, in the night, are raised questioning voices: What meaning is there without tradition, custom, continuity, culture? What hope, without a plan? What purpose, without a goal or design?

The pointed, red triangular structure, with a whitish brown patch, hovering just to the left of the moon . . .

The aerial box beside the billowing yellow and violet net, intersected by the 27.95 metres long copper and painted steel structure, groaning now, steel on steel, in the 25 kilometre per hour wind from south-southwest . . .

The colour gold registers only on a particular eye, only within a singular mind, only for an instant, the description of which is obsolete even as it occurs.

I have spent a long time considering the forms these aerial heterarchies assume. There is no real hierarchical form, because each performer is autonomous, each structure unique, each movement complex, unrepeatable. These performers do, however, comprise a community, because in some ways they are working together. The forms this community assumes are a result of a complicated interaction of spontaneity, planned manoeuvring and highly variable atmospheric conditions. The point is this: the results appear random and without visual coherence, as classically determined, as predetermined by adherence to conventional models. The idea of community as traditionally defined, in terms of a coherence visibly apparent, appears now to dissolve within a more complex form of order, a fluid-dynamical order.

From below, in the ancient and modern city of Paris, the aerial structures appear as just another exhibition — gypsy objects of fascination, invasion, or wonder.

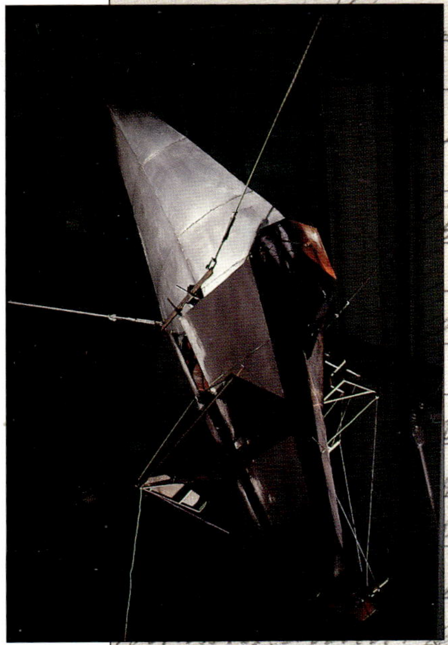

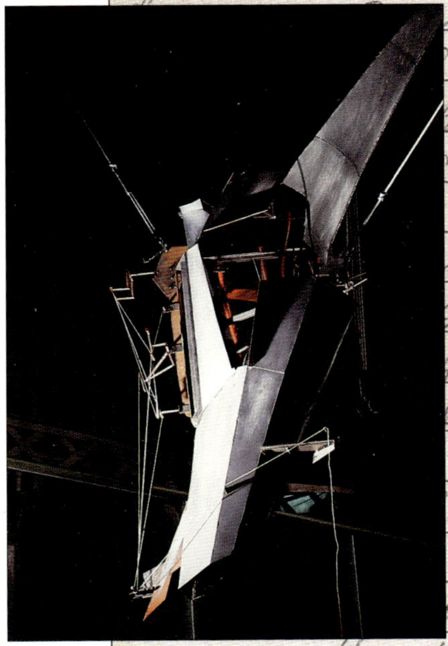

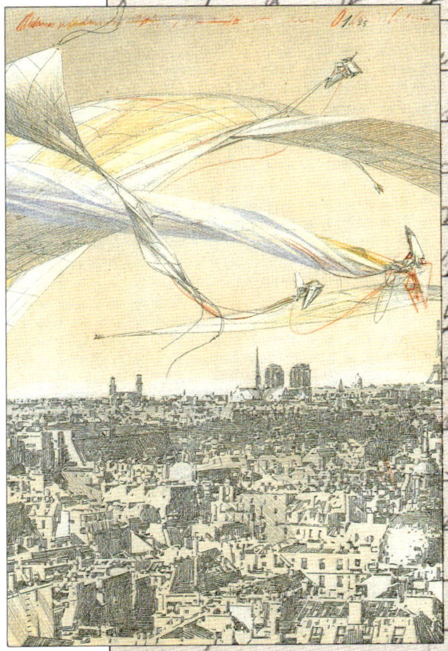

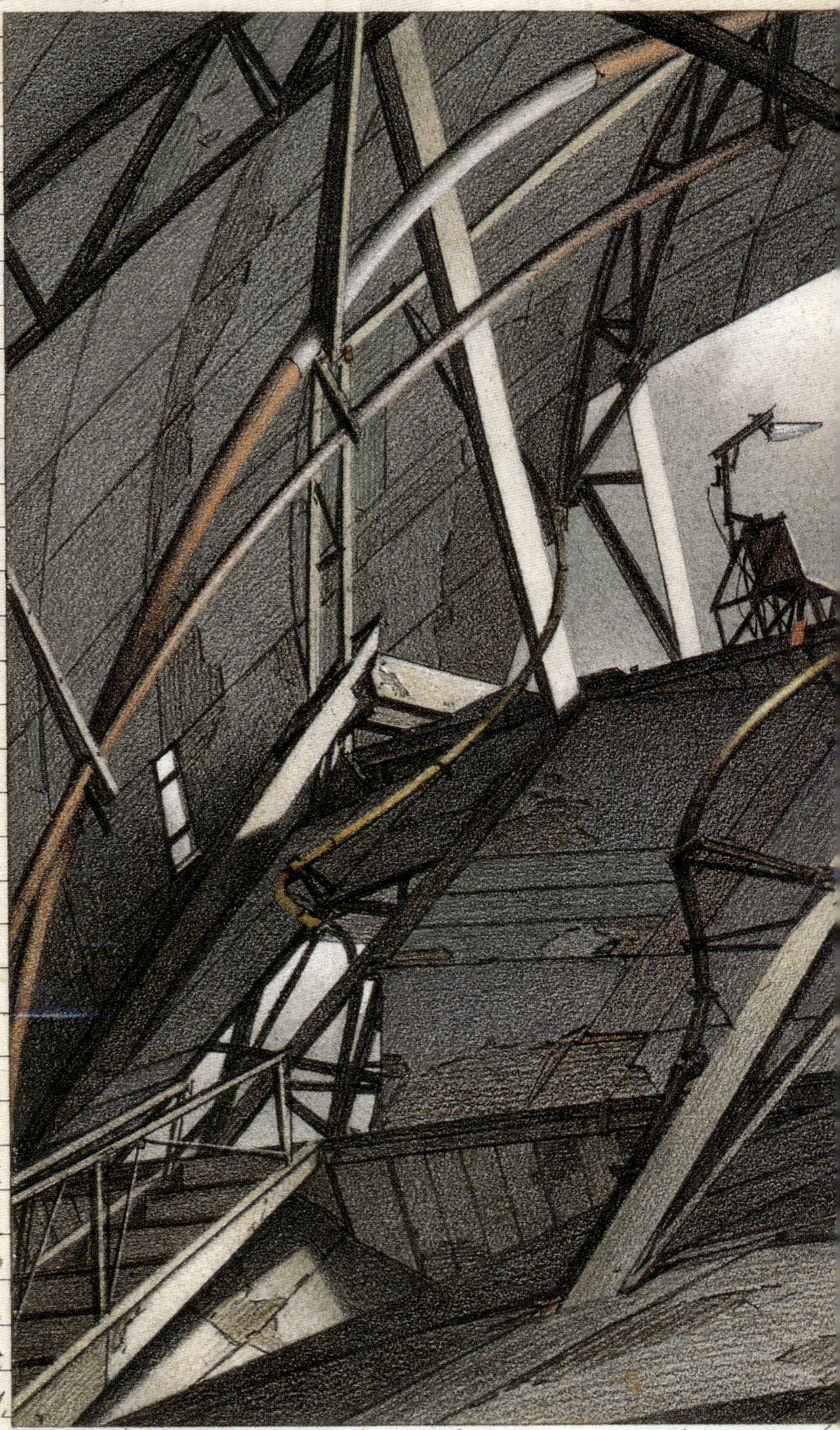

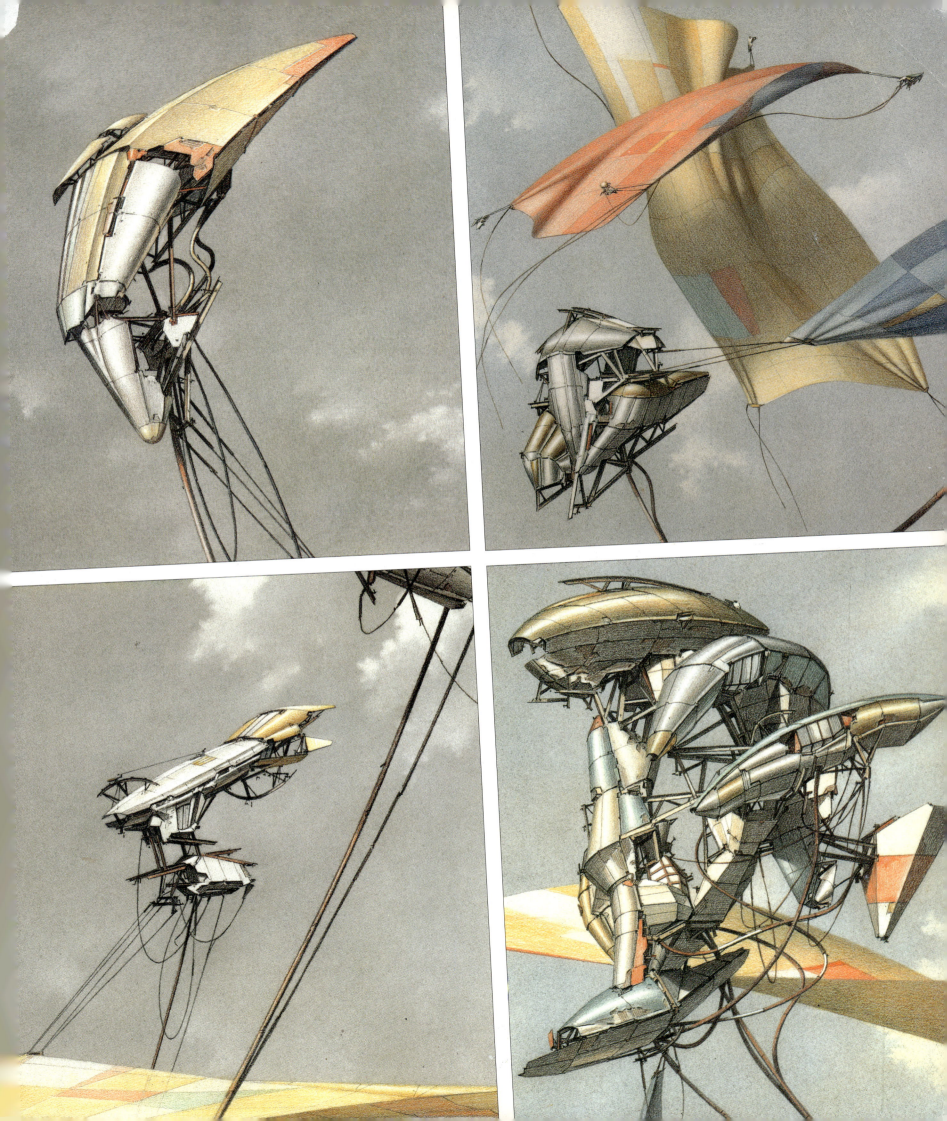

STATIONS

84

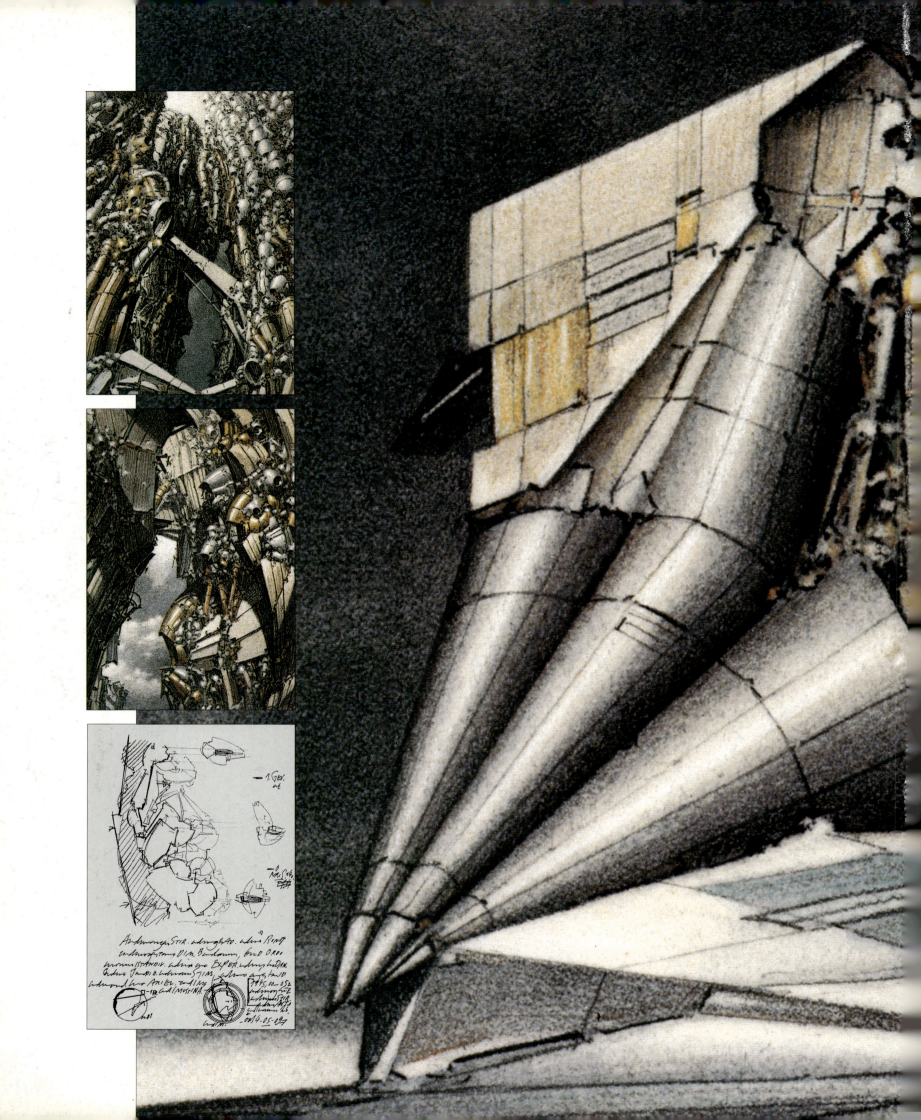

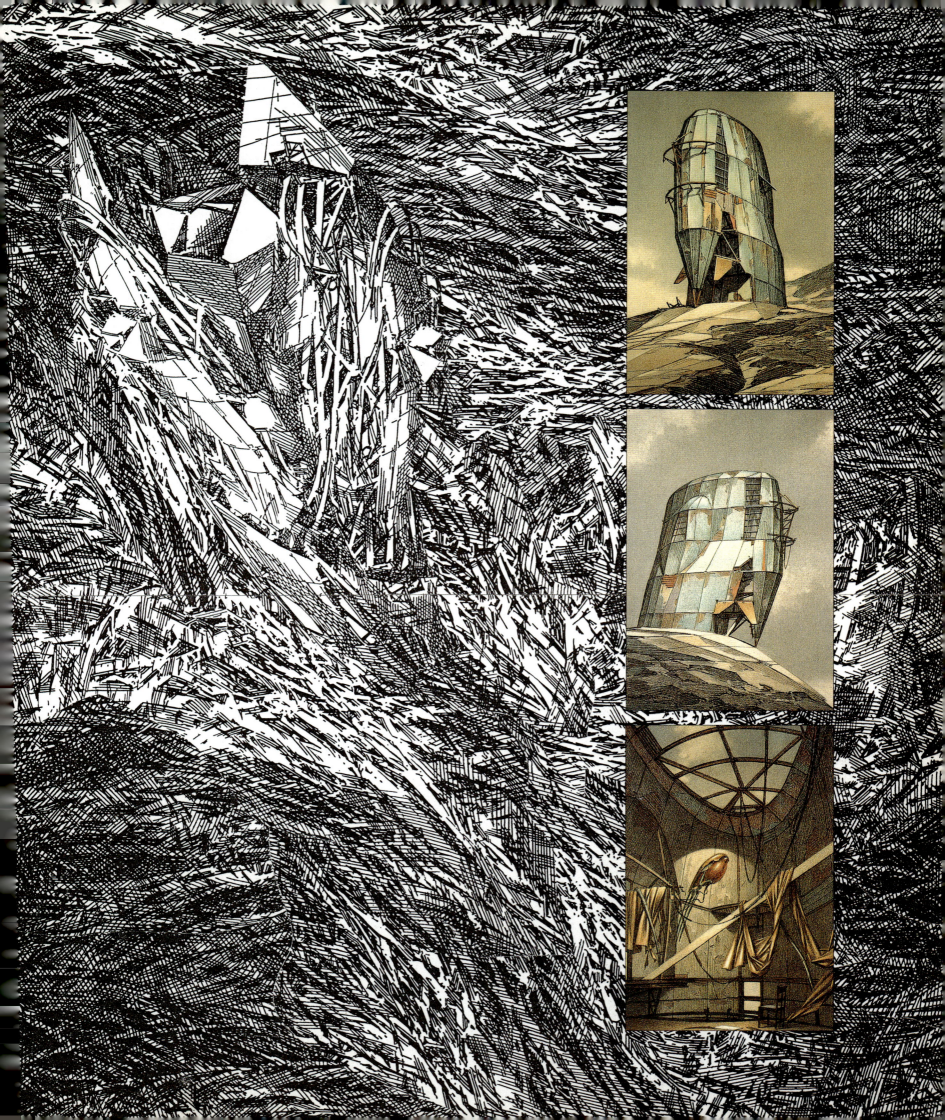

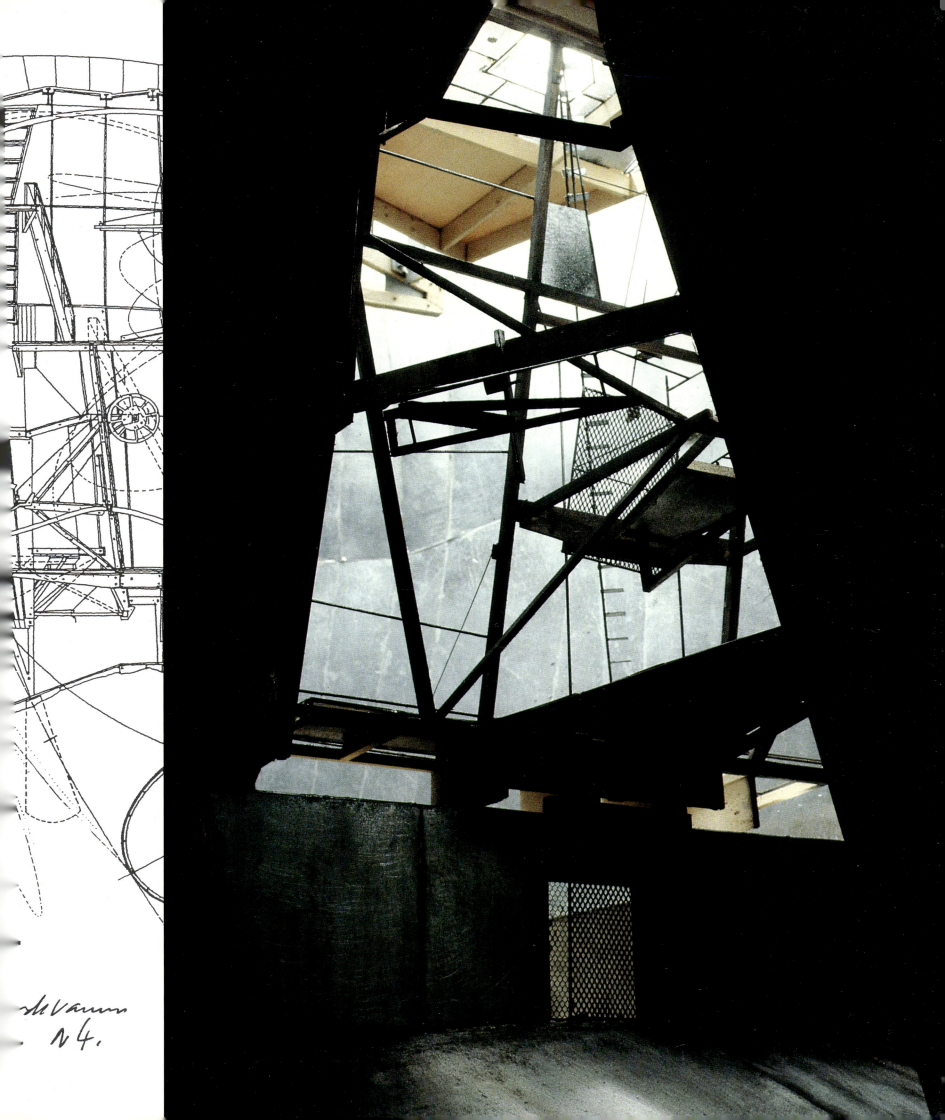

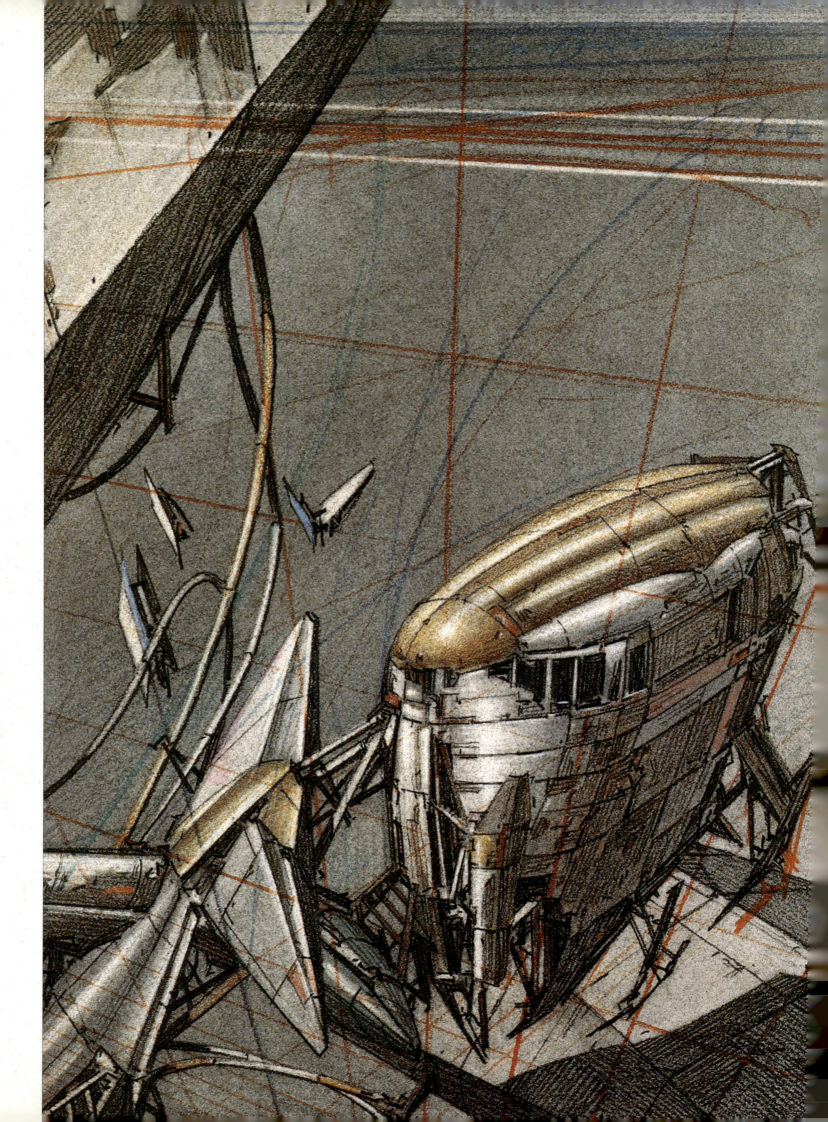

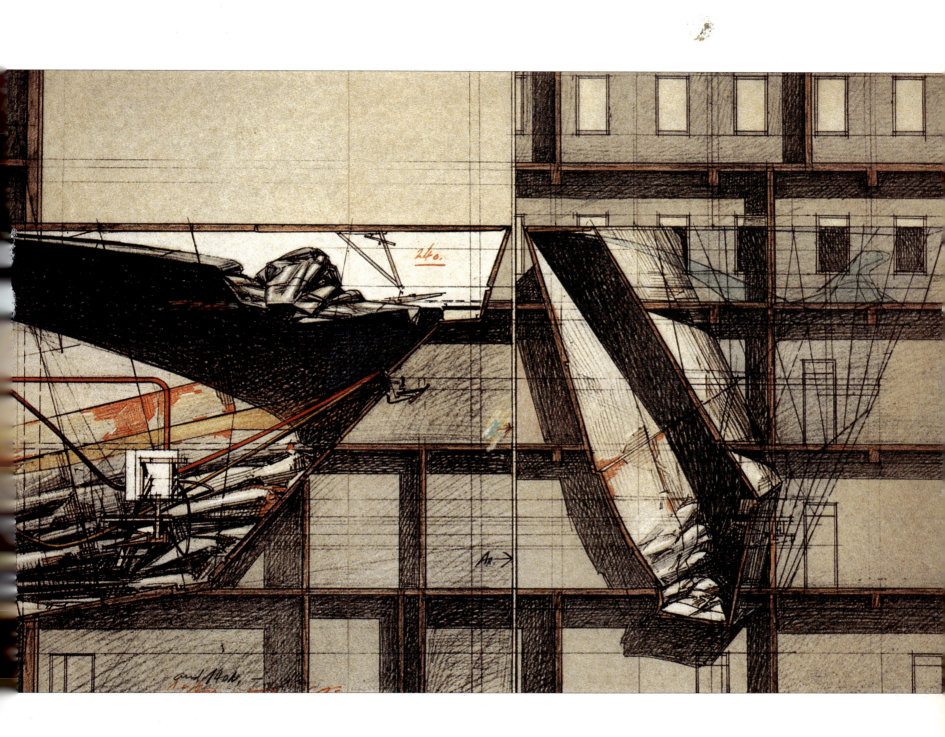

SUPROTNA MASA JE

OPPOSING MASS IS

SISTEM 9 8 75 8 0 0 0 0 0

SYSTEM

POLOVINA, EKSPLODIRAJ, ČETVRTINA

HALF, EXPLODE, ONE-FOURTH

5 Y 6 0 0 0 0 7 9 4 OTVORENO!

OPEN

I JOŠ JEDAN S

AND ANOTHER WITH

0 0 8 5 2 0 0 9 5 4 0 0 8 LET FLIGHT

ČUVAJ SVE STROJEVE

MJERA!

SAVE ALL MACHINES

7 9 7 8 0 0 8

MEASURE

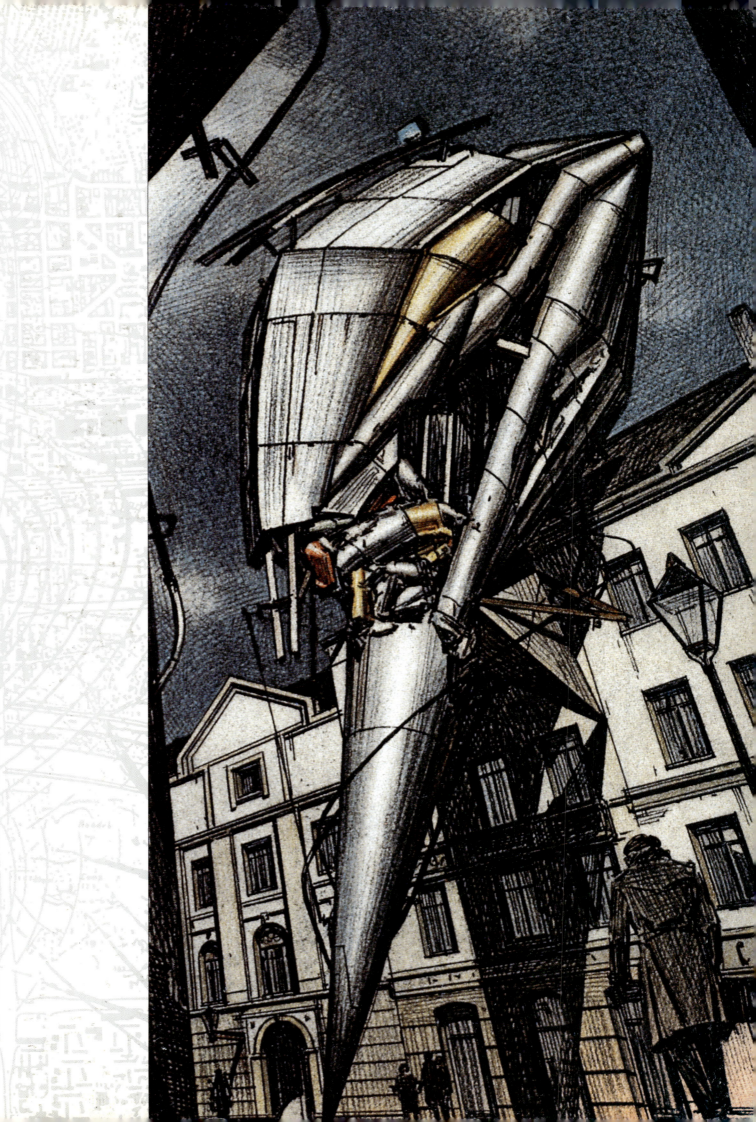

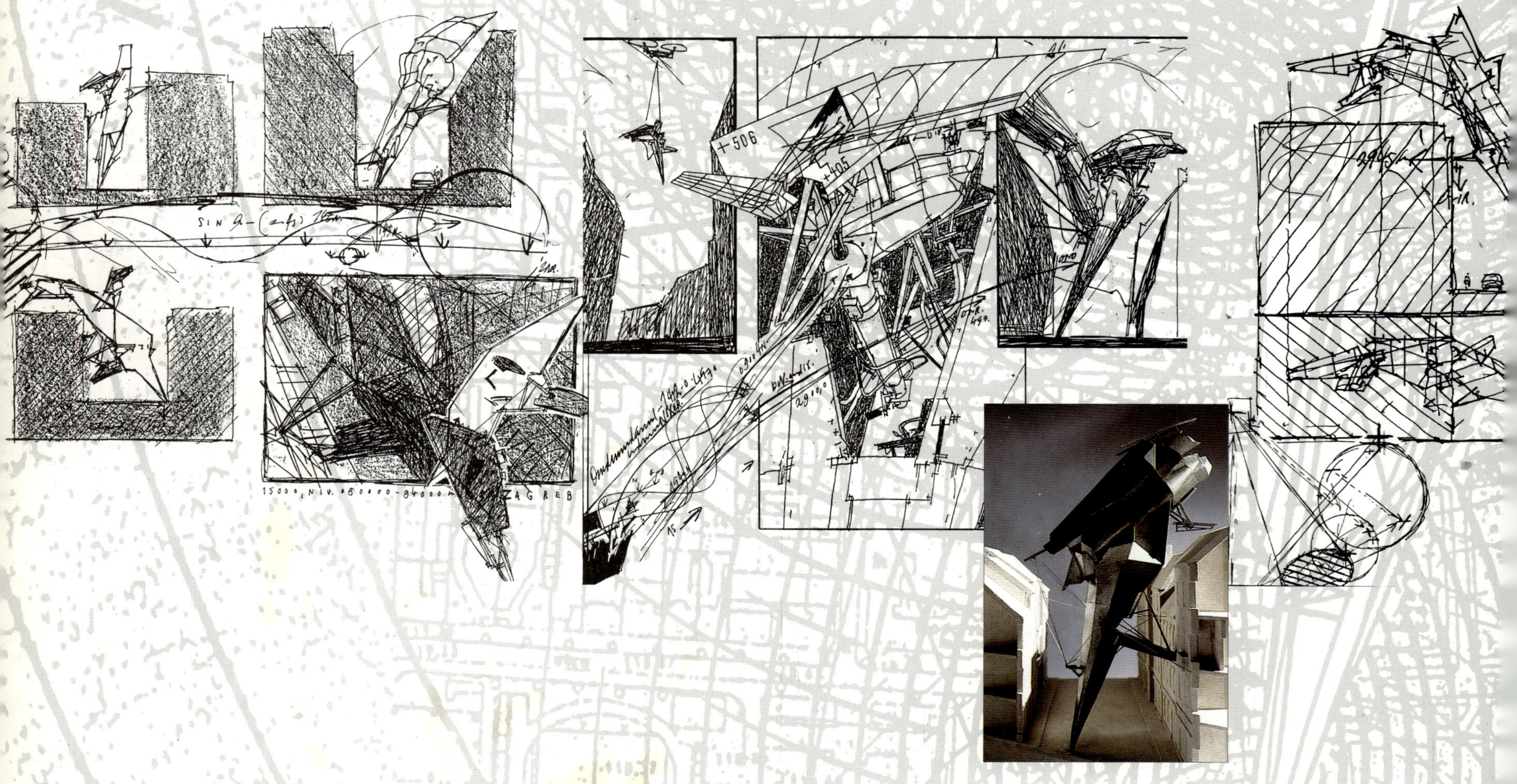
+506
ZAGREB

122

126

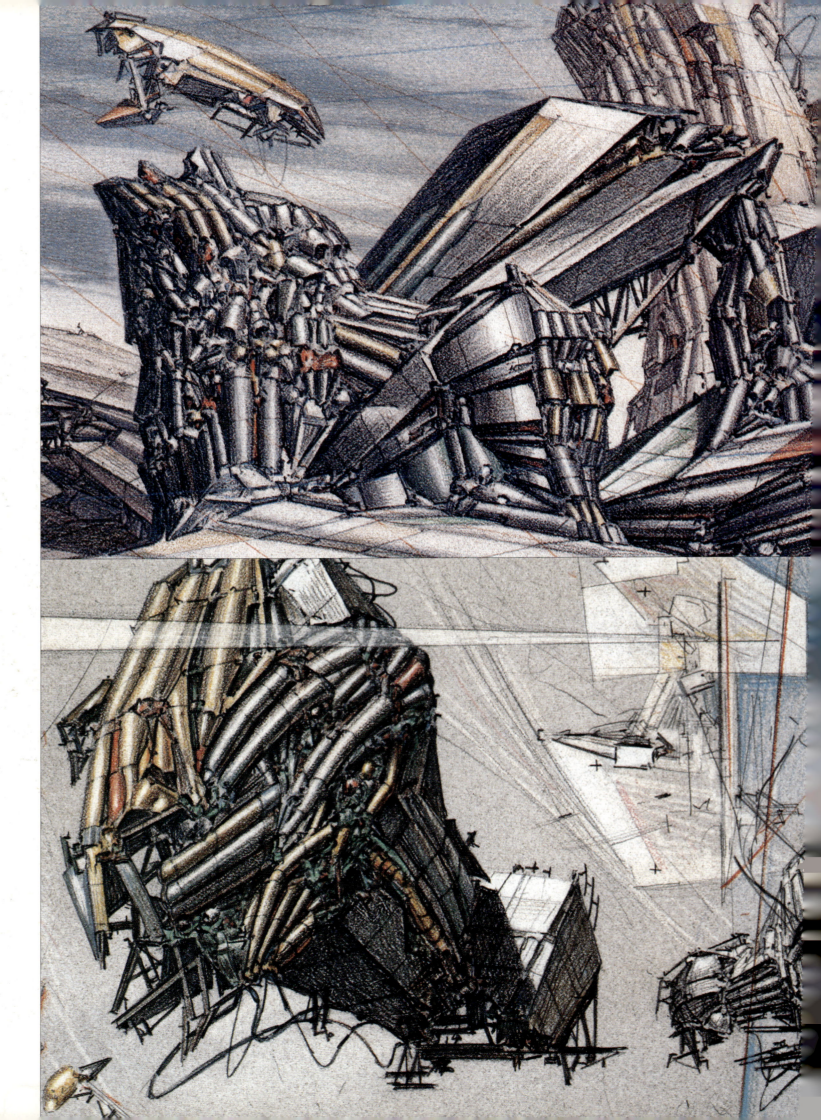

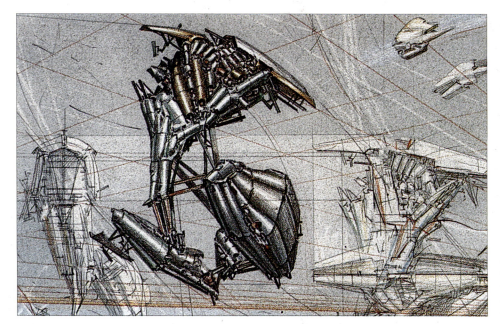

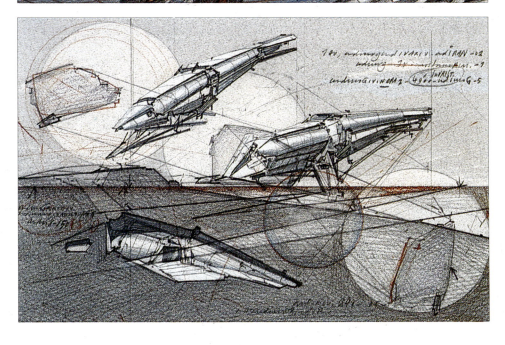

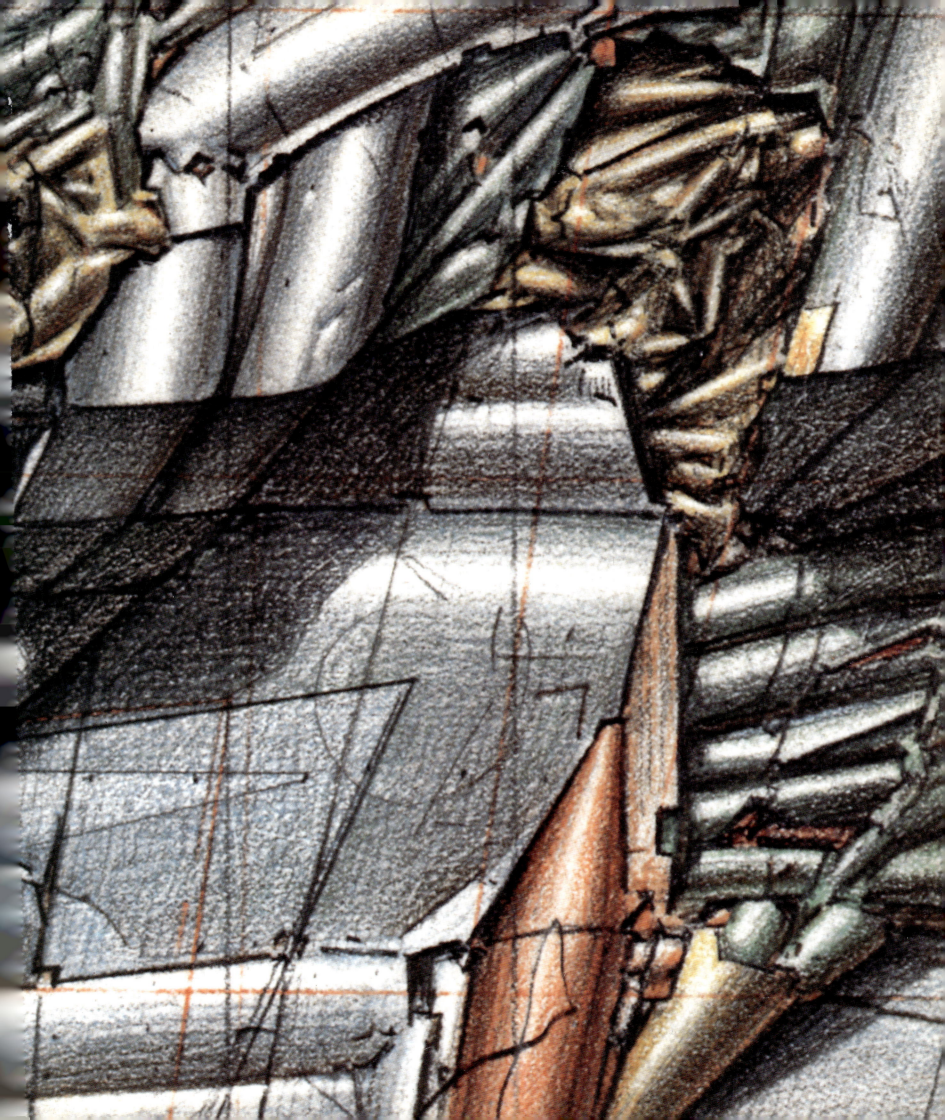

DOUBLE LANDSCAPE, VIENNA

Architecture is a political act. The long version: *all innovative architecture engages ethical issues that have profound political consequences.* Such is the case with the Terrace-plateau project for the Museum for Applied Arts in Vienna, designed by its director, the architect Peter Noever. His struggle against political authority, but also against architects and the inertia of established taste, resulted in the construction of a monumental structure that at once transforms and seeks transformation.

The Terrace-plateau is a new ground, fertile in its emptiness. By virtue of its intercession, the court-yard of the Museum is re-formed, set into a new degree and quality of motion — with resolve, but without resolution. The first lone figures appearing on its surface inevitably reduce its eloquence. From being a grand stage of harrowing, existential solitude, the first strolling tourists reduce the great cantilevered platform and flank of steps to a mere convey-ance and convenience. Then — and only then — is something more forceful required.

It is not too soon to propose an even newer re-formation, to challenge the new *status quo*, and precisely to save the terrace-plateau from that position, so antithetical to the spirit of its inception and presence. By a doubling and redoubling of surfaces, a new, composite terrain is brought into being, a redundancy evoking not an emptiness so much as the as yet unused potentiality offered by a more complex order.

Is existence only to be one long potentiality, never to be used, one interminable possibility, never to be realised, given a final identity and name? Can the wanderer find no home, no place of comfort, of rest and recuperation? Is it all just a relentless going on and on, until going on is abruptly interrupted by death?

What must be avoided at the Terrace-plateau in Vienna is exactly what must be avoided by the museum itself — that it becomes a pedestal for 'works of art'. This eventuality posits a false completeness, degrading to both the institution and the works it presents. The visitors to the museum, who might stroll out onto the great, raised terrace, must not find there a satisfying object, a thing that com-pletes and justifies their visit and journey. The Terrace-plateau, with its impossible cantilever, wants to fly. In its struggle against the gravity of earth, and of history, it wants to begin, and never end.

It is exactly this instinct for un-boundedness that threatens a *status quo* in Vienna, a city thriving and surviving on the discreteness of its *objets d'art*.

The new structure to be constructed on the back of the Terrace-plateau doubles its weight, and thereby its impetus to fly, by an inverse logic of inertia: the more it is pressed to earth, the more energy it gains to extend itself deeply into unbounded space.

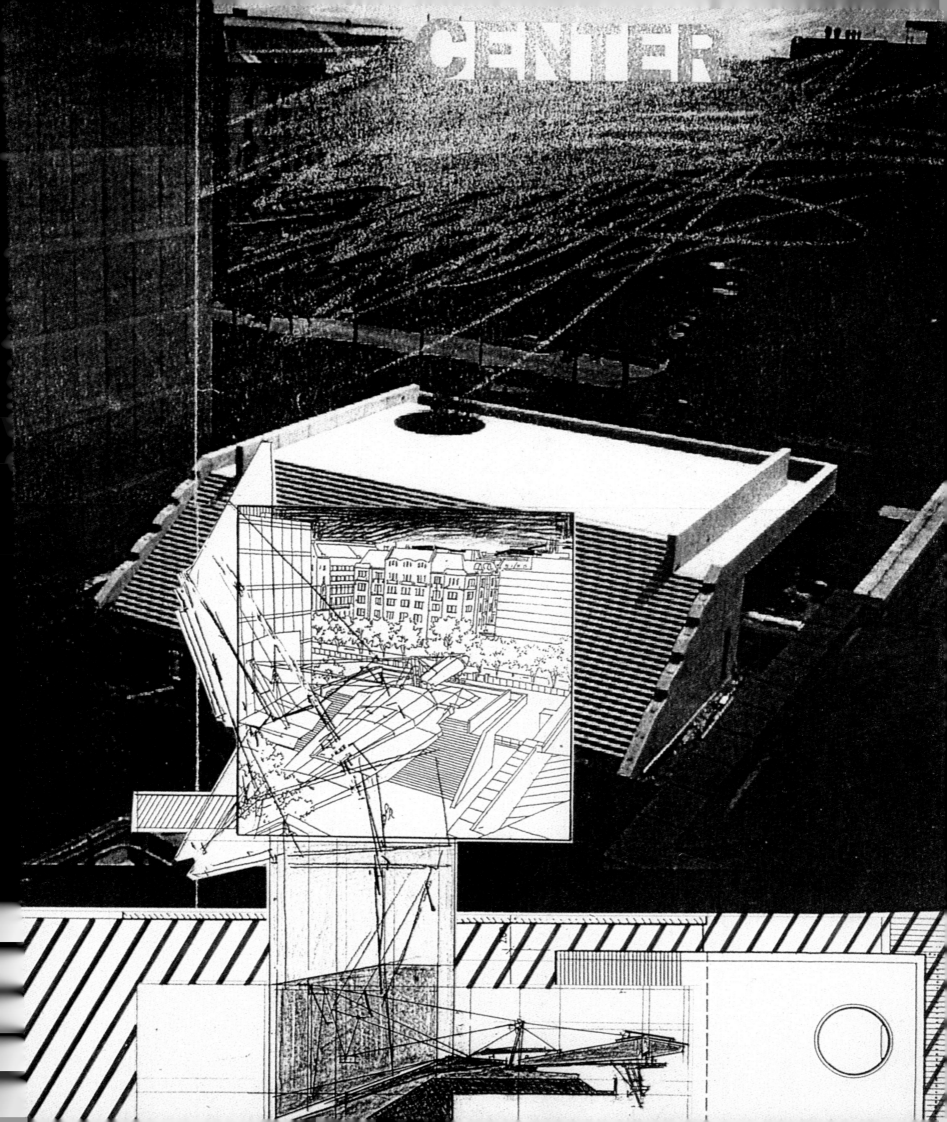

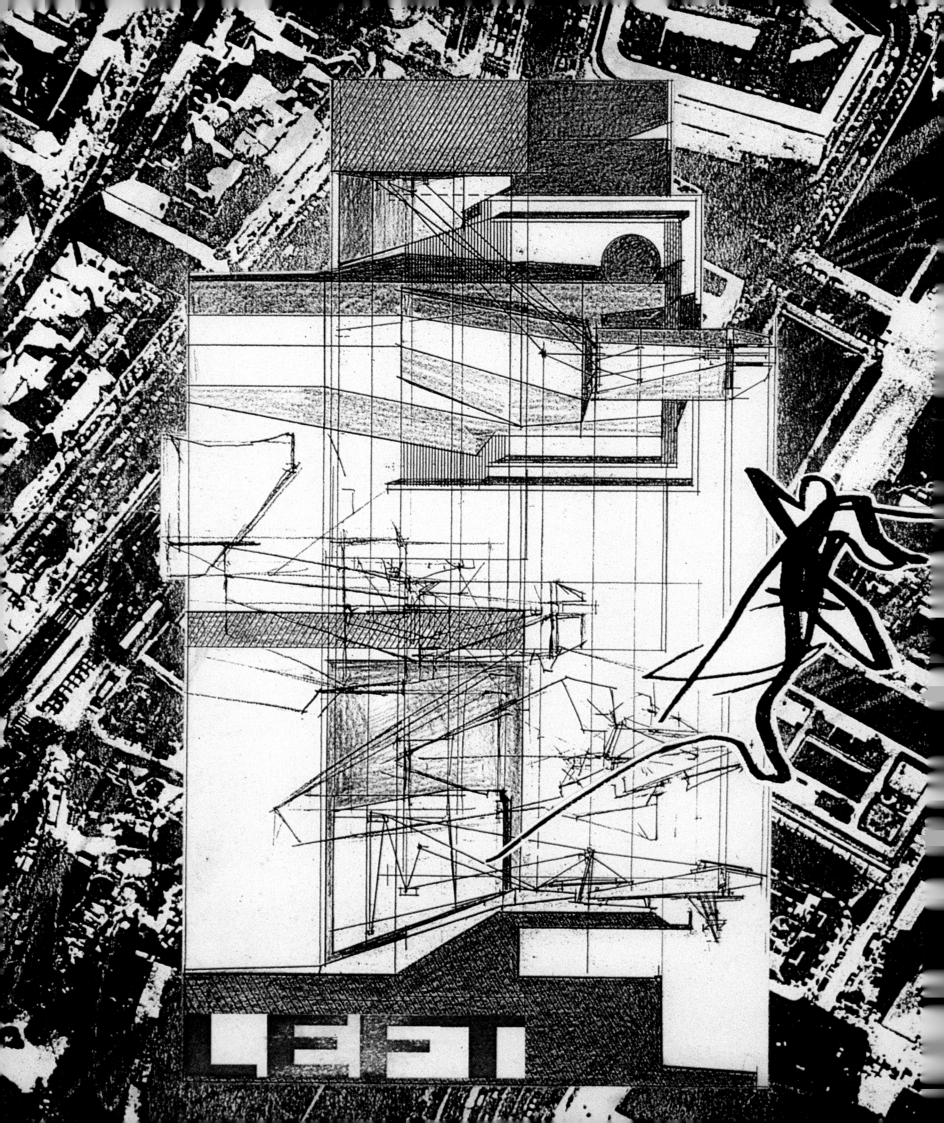

RIGHT

GLOSSARY

FREEDOM: a state emptied of preconceived value, use, function, meaning; an extreme state of loss within which choice is unavoidable; a condition of maximum potential, realised fully in the present moment. **CHOICE:** the act made necessary by acute awareness of the present moment; involves risk. **CYBERNETICS:** a system of thought and action which excludes nothing, does not contain anything or include everything; mind/machine relationships, hence human/extra-human interactions. **RECURSION:** a condition of circular repetition, the input-output states of which are self-transforming. **CIRCUS:** a cybernetic state of free interactions; a community of autonomous performers, continuously re-formed by the independent choice of each; a feedback loop, a recursive mechanism. **FEEDBACK:** the input-output process; the mechanism of self-transformation; the result of dialogue, interaction, choice; a state of unpredictability. **UNIVERSCIENCE:** a transdisciplinary field of work and study based on the relationship of cognitive processes to the phenomenology of light; a body of principles relevant to architecture, based on the interplay of metrical systems defining boundaries of evolving form. **KNOWLEDGE:** the invention of the world in all the complexity and multiplicity of its phenomena. **ARCHITECTURE:** instrument for the invention of knowledge through action; the invention of invention. **DIGITAL COMPUTER:** a fast counting machine — nothing more, nothing less. **BIOLOGICAL COMPUTER:** the human brain; the most unpredictable, hence most complex computer known. **DETERMINATE FIELD:** geometrical field predetermined by a self-consistent set of rules of operation, eg, the Cartesian field. **FREEFIELD:** geometrical field unpredictably determined by the complex flux of conditions within the field, eg, the field of non-linear systems. **LIVING-LABORATORY:** architecture for living and working experimentally. **HIERARCHY:** a predetermined vertical chain of authority that works from the top down. **HETERARCHY:** a spontaneous lateral network of autonomous individuals; a system of authority based on the evolving performances of individuals, eg, a cybernetic circus. **NETWORK:** an ephemeral, freely-evolving, unpredictable, dynamical four-dimensional pattern. **PHENOMENON:** a description of an experience. **EXISTENTIAL:** a principle of thought affirming itself in action; existence confirming itself. **GEOMAGNETIC LIFT:** the principle of levitating masses by their interaction with the earth's ambient electromagnetic fields. **CONSTRUCTION:** the invention of reality. **REALITY:** a state necessitating the invention of construction. **OBJECTIVE/SUBJECTIVE:** terms of a dualism divorcing experience from reality. **CAUSALITY:** a hierarchical description of reality; preconceived chain of phenomena comprising a determinate field. **FUNCTION:** the present feedback mechanism of a phenomenon or construction. **COMMUNICATION:** an exchange of knowledge between autonomous individuals. **AUTONOMY:** the essential condition of freedom; organic unity, hence the source of the individual's existential isolation; distinction by virtue of boundary. **DIALECTIC:** free dialogue among autonomous individuals. **INDIGESTIBILITY:** resistance to being consumed by a system; a characteristic of freedom. **ENTROPY:** consequence of the 'second law' of thermodynamics; predicted inevitable loss of energy, individuality, descriptiveness and ability to describe. **BEAUTY:** 'knowledge without interest'; ideas embodied in and transcended by forms. **PHYSICALITY:** the state of all present conditions; definition of quantifiable phenomena; matrix of reality. **NOW:** precisely of the present moment; the space of reality; the field of phenomena bounded by description. **INDIVIDUAL:** human embodiment of autonomous being; inventor of the world. **CHAOS:** state of maximum entropy. **ORDER:** a matrix of distinctions, itself uniquely distinct. **DIALOGUE:** communications with a heterarchy. **MONOLOGUE:** communications within a hierarchy. **ASSERTION:** an intention stated *a posteriori* to a result of action; an experimental finding. **KINEMATICS:** a system describing precise relationships of action. **USE:** the act of inventing. **PROGRAMME:** preconception of present conditions and results; predetermination of the present moment. **PROBABILITY:** the phenomenon and spontaneous inevitability. **MEANING:** the free interaction of values. **DYNAMICS:** a system describing an underlying impetus to action. **QUANTUM THEORY:** paradox of energy/matter relationships. **QUANTUM MECHANICS:** kinematics of ambiguous observed/observer relationships. **RELATIVITY THEORY:** the great destroyer of hierarchies; description of the world according to an observer. **ONTOLOGY:** the study of being — static and hierarchical. **ONTOGENETICS:** the study of becoming, dynamic and heterarchical. **EXPERIENCE:** transformation of reality through perception. **FREESPACE:** a construction free of preconceived value, use or meaning; an element in a heterarchy. **FREE-ZONE:** heterarchy of freespaces; pattern of urban order based on knowledge and performance; a system opposing mass culture; a subversion of hierarchies. **SELF-REFERENTIALITY:** a paradox of the self; phenomenon including its own description of itself; condition of freedom and heterarchy. **CONSUMERISM:** a state of becoming limited by the total entropy of a system. **MASS CULTURE:** a system diminishing the autonomy of individuals; a state of undifferentiated nature within which the making of distinctions is difficult. **REVOLUTION:** self-cancelling mass political machinations; the necessity of formlessness. **REBELLION:** individual resistance to established form. **MODERN:** of the present moment. **CONTEXT:** matrix of bounding relationships. **FORM:** the condition of boundaries, perceived as exterior to self. **SPACE:** the condition of boundaries, perceived as interior to self. **EXPERIMENT:** action without goal, undertaken for itself. **DRAWING:** making marks by a process of mind-hand-eye coordination; an act of building; an action indispensable to architecture. **STRUGGLE:** the essential condition of freedom.

LEBBEUS WOODS Born in 1940, in Lansing, Michigan, USA; educated at the University of Illinois (Architecture) and Purdue University (Engineering). Worked for Eero Saarinen and Associates on the John Deere and Ford Foundation Headquarters Building projects, then in private practice. Turned to theory and experimental projects since 1976. Co-founded the New York-based Research Institute for Experimental Architecture. He has been a Visiting Professor at Harvard and Columbia Universities, and is currently Visiting Professor of Architecture at The Cooper Union in New York.

SELECTED EXHIBITIONS: One Person 1982 *AEON: The Architecture of Time*, Express/Network Gallery, New York. Travelled to University of Illinois School of Architecture, Champaign-Urbana. **1984** *CENTRES: Three Public Building Projects*, Storefront for Art and Architecture, New York. **1985** *Architecture: The Mythic Journey*, The Indianapolis Museum of Art. *Origins*, The Architectural Association, London; travelled to Van Rooy Galerie, Amsterdam. **1987** *Centricity: The Unified Urban Field*, Aedos Galerie, Berlin, Catalogue; travelled to Stuttgart Association of Architects Galerie; University of Siogen, Germany; Storefront for Art and Architecture, New York. *Cyclical Cities*, Rom Galerie, Oslo, Norway; travelled to Skala Galerie, Copenhagen. **1988** *Underground Berlin*, The Art and Architecture Exhibition Space (2AES), San Francisco. **1989** *Terra Nova*, Fenster Galerie, Frankfurt am Main, Germany. **1991** *Berlin-Free-Zone*, Aedes Galerie, Berlin. Catalogue. *Zagreb-Free-Zone*, Museum of Arts and Crafts, Zagreb, Croatia. Catalogue. *Lebbeus Woods: Architecture*, Galerie Dessa, Ljubljana, Slovenia. *Centric 44: Lebbeus Woods*, University Art Museum, California State University, Long Beach. Catalogue. *Architecture is a Political Act*, Gund Hall Gallery, Harvard University, Cambridge, Massachusetts.
Group 1979 *New Americans*, Villa Trajan, Rome. **1980** *Young Architects*, Yale University School of Architecture Gallery, New Haven, Connecticut. Catalogue. *Tribune Tower Competition* - Late Entries, Museum of Contemporary Art, Chicago. Catalogue. **1983** *Juxtapositions*, PS1, Institute for Art and Urban Resources, New York. **1984** *Adam's House in Paradise*, Storefront for Art and Architecture, New York. Catalogue. **1986** *Vision der Moderne*, Deutsches Architekturmuseum, Frankfurt am Main, Catalogue. *Via New York*, Sloan Gallery, Mexico City. **1987** *Zauber der Meduse*, Kunstlerhaus, Vienna, Catalogue. **1988** *Berlin: Denkmal oder Denkmodell*, Kunsthalle, Berlin. Travelled to Pavilion de L'Arsenal, Paris; Bern Museum of Art; Krakow Museum of Fine Arts; Kiev Fine Arts museum; Moscow Society of Architects. Catalogue. *DMZ*, Storefront for Art and Architecture, New York. Catalogue. **1989** *Kunstlerhauser*, Deutsches Architecturmuseum, Frankfurt am Main. Catalogue. *Paris: Architecture et Utopie*, Pavilion de L'Arsenal, Paris. Travelled to Kunsthalle, Berlin. Catalogue. **1990** *RIEA: The First Conference*, Aedes Galerie, Berlin. Catalogue.

SELECTED WRITINGS: Monographs *Architecture, Sculpture, Painting Series*, Xenon Press, 1979. **Einstein Tomb**, Pamphlet Architecture 6, 1980. **AEON: The Architecture of Time**, Express Extra Edition, 1982. **Centers**, Storefront Press, 1984. **Origins**, The Architectural Association, London, 1985. **Centricity**, Aedes Editions, Berlin, 1987. **OneFiveFour**, Princeton Architectural Press, New York, 1989. **Lebbeus Woods: Terra Nova**, A+U Extra Edition, Tokyo, 1991. **The New City**, Simon and Schustor, New York, 1992. **Writings by Lebbeus Woods** **Express**, Vol 1, No 2, April 1981, cover illustration. 'La Casa e le Cose', **Gran Bazaar**, August 1981, p 147-149. 'California Counterpoint', **Express**, Vol 3, No 1, August-September 1983, p 4-5. 'Architecture, Consciousness and the Mythos of Time', **AA Files**, Number 7, September 1984, p 3-13. 'Projects: Lebbeus Woods', **A+U**, Tokyo, February 1985, p 81-88. 'Centre for New Technology', **Architecture and Abstraction**, Pratt Institute/Rizzoli, New York, Fall 1985, p 66-68. 'The Impertinent Genius of Peter Cook', **Architectures**, No 2, 1986, p 1986, p 16-19. 'Project: Epicyclarium', **A+U**, Tokyo, May 1987, p 81-88. 'Exhibition: Zaha Hadid. The Tension Builds', **A+U**, Tokyo, September, 1987, p 4-5. 'A Cooking Lesson. Exhibition of the Drawings and Models of Peter Cook', **A+U**, June, 1987, p 7-8. 'Building Projects: Macdonald and Salter', **Front 2**, Storefront for Art and Architecture, 1987, p 2. 'Henley and the Enigma of Michael Webb', **Temple Island**, Mega V, The Architectural Association, London, 1987, p 53-56. 'Gilbert, Nishimoto, Park: Three Projects', **Sites**, Fall 1987, p 49-65. 'Centricity', **Places**, A Quarterly Journal of Environmental Design, Berkeley/MIT Press, Vol 5, No 3, Summer, 1988, p 84-89. 'Terra Nova', **Front 3**, Storefront for Art and Architecture, New York, 1988, 46-47. 'Peter Cook and Christine Hawley: An Epilogue', *El Croquis* 39, April/May 1989, p 40. 'Brave New City: Lebbeus Woods' Underground Berlin,', **Interview**, Vol XIX, No 1, January 1989 p 58-61. 'Experimental Architecture: A Commentary', *Avant Garde 2*, University of Colorado, Summer, 1989, p 6-19. 'Model City: A Project by the American Architect Michael Sorkin', **A+U**, Tokyo, September, 1989, p 9-12. 'Present Tense', **OZ, Journal of Architecture and Design**, Kansas State University, Vol 12, 1990, p 52-55. 'Berlin Subterraneo', **ARDI**, Barcelona, Vol 14, March/April, 1990, p 88-99. 'What Does it Mean?', **RIEA: The First Conference**, New York/Berlin, Princeton Architectural Press/Aedes, 1990, p 2-3, and 'Terra Nova', p 47-51. 'Neil Denari's Philosophical Machines', **A+U**, Tokyo, March 1991, p 43-44. 'Berlin-Free-Zone', **Skala**, No 24-25, 1991, p 24-29. 'Zagreb-Free-Zone: Heterarchy of Urban Form and Architecture', **Avant Garde 5**, University of Colorado, Winter 1991, p 72-103. 'Heterarchy of Urban Form and Architecture', **Architectural Design, Free Space Architecture**, Academy Editions, London, March/April 1992, p 36-53. 'Terra Nova', **Architecture in Transition** (P Noever, Ed), Prestel Verlag, Munich, 1991, p 133-151. 'Lauretta Vinciarelli: The Architecture of Light', **A+U**, Tokyo, (Forthcoming, May 1992). 'Destroy Experimental Architecture!' **OZ, Journal of Architecture and Design**, Kansas State University, (Forthcoming, Fall 1992). 'Antigravity Houses', **Wombat**, Todo Press, Tokyo, (Forthcoming May 1992). **Selected Bibliography** Betsky, Aaron, **Violated Perfection: Architecture and the Fragmentation of the Modern**, Rizzoli, New York, 1990, p 176-181. Brown, Olive, 'Lebbeus Woods. Projets au Futur,' **Crée/Architecture Intérieure**, Paris, March-April 1985, p 81-88. Coma, Dan, 'The Projects of Lebbeus Woods,' **A+U**, Tokyo, May, 1985, p 81-88. Cook, Peter and Llewellyn-Jones, Rosie (editors), **New Spirit in Architecture**, New York, Rizzoli, 1991, p 40-43. Games, Stephen, 'Dream Cities,' **AA Files**, The Architectural Association, London, Spring 1986, p 82-86. Jonak, Ulf, **Sturz and Riss**, Friedrich Viewweg & Sohn, Braunschweig/Weisbaden, 1989, p 93-99. Lacy, Bill N (editor), **100 Contemporary Architects: Drawings and Sketches**, Harry N Abrams, New York, 1991, frontispiece, p 40-43. Norten, Enrique, 'Proyectos y dibujos de Lebbeus Woods,' **Arquitectura**, No 2, Mexico City/Verano, 1991, p 24-29. **Progressive Architecture** (editors), 'Environmental Theatre', January 1974, cover, p 88-89. Rochon, Richard and Linton, Harold, **Colour in Architectural Illustration**, Van Nostrand Reinhold, 1988, p 140-146. Slavin, Maeve, 'Shooting Stars: Lebbeus Woods', **Interiors**, May 1985, p 304-305. Sorkin, Michael, 'Brave New Worlds', **Architectural Record**, February, 1980, p 80-83. ——, 'Architecture Rising: Lebbeus Woods' Projekt Aerial Paris,' **Daidalos**, Berlin, September 1990, p 119-121. ——, **Exquisite Corpse**, Verso, New York, 1991, p 266-270. Stein, Kathleen, 'Castles in the Air,' **Omni**, New York, July 1986, p 36-38, 91-94. Thau, Carsten, 'Arkitekti Atlantis', **Skala**, No 14, May 1988, p 14-17. ——, 'Lebbeus Woods Interview,' **Skala**, No 14, May 1988, p 14-17. Thomsen, Christian W, 'Lebbeus Woods, RIEA and its Berlin Exhibition of Experimental Architecture,' **A+U**, Tokyo, October 1990, p 30-40. ——, **Literarchitektur**, Dumont Verlag, Koln, 1990, p 130-132, 144-145, 176, 185. ——, **Experimentelle Architekten der Gegenwart**, Dumont Verlag, Koln, 1991. ——, 'Vision für Berlin,' **Ambiente**, Die Kunst Zu Leben, Munich, October 1988, p 58-82. Vukio, Fedja, 'Der Kampf um Freiraume (The Fight for Freezones)', **Umriss**, No 1/2, Vienna, 1992, p 57-59. ——, 'Vizualni dnevnik kosmara', **Vjesnik**, Zagreb, 19 July 1991, cover, p 10-15. Wagner, Aleksandra, 'Stranac u republici Sarajevo', **Nasi Dani**, No 1018, Sarajevo, 25 June 1991.

SELECTED PROJECTS: 1974 Environmental Theatre. **1975** Four Houses. **1977** Simultaneous City, Wall Fragments. **1978** Architecture-Sculpture-Painting Series. **1979** Four Ceremonial Constructions, City in Time. **1980** Einstein Tomb, Four Houses (Second Version). **1981** Four Cities. **1982-83** AEON. **1984** Epicyclarium. **1985** A City, Sector 1576N, Centre for New Technology. **1986** Cyclical Cities. **1987** Centricity, Aerial Structures. **1988** Underground Berlin, DMZ. **1989** Aerial Paris, Solohouse. **1990** Stations, Berlin-Free-Zone. **1991** Zagreb-Free-Zone, Freespace Structures, Icebergs, Double Landscape (Vienna), Antigravity Houses.